M000104971

COMMON CORE ACHIEVE

Mastering Essential Test Readiness Skills

GED® Test Exercise Book

SCIENCE

Mc Graw Hill Education

Bothell, WA • Chicago, IL • Columbus, OH • New York, NY

GED®, GED TESTING SERVICE®, and GED PLUS® are registered trademarks owned by American Council on Education ("ACE"). This material is not endorsed or approved by ACE or the GED Testing Service LLC.

MHEonline.com

Copyright © 2015 McGraw-Hill Education

All rights reserved. No part of this publication may be reproduced or distributed in any form or by any means, or stored in a database or retrieval system, without the prior written consent of McGraw-Hill Education, including, but not limited to, network storage or transmission, or broadcast for distance learning.

Send all inquiries to:
McGraw-Hill Education
8787 Orion Place
Columbus, OH 43240

ISBN: 978-0-02-135572-3
MHID: 0-02-135572-X

Printed in the United States of America.

3 4 5 6 7 8 9 RHR 17 16 15 14

Table of Contents

Congratulations! If you are using this book, it means that you are taking a key step toward achieving an important new goal for yourself. You are preparing to take the GED® Test, one of the most important steps in the pathway toward career, educational, and lifelong well-being and success.

Common Core Achieve: Mastering Essential Test Readiness Skills is designed to help you learn or strengthen the skills you will need when you take the GED® Test. The Science Exercise Book provides you with additional practice of the key concepts, core skills, and core practices required for success on test day and beyond.

How to Use This Book

This book is designed to follow the same lesson structure as the Core Student Module. Each lesson in the Science Exercise Book is broken down into the same sections as the core module, with a page or more devoted to the key concepts covered in each section. Each lesson contains at least one Test-Taking Tip, which helps you prepare for a test by giving you hints such as how to approach certain question types, or strategies such as how to eliminate unnecessary information. At the back of this book, you will find the answer key for each lesson. The answer to each question is provided along with a rationale for why the answer is correct. If you get an answer incorrect, please return to the appropriate lesson and section in either the online or print Core Student Module to review the specific content.

There is one additional resource at the back of this book to further help you. The Calculator Reference Sheet shows you how to use the TI-30XS MultiView™ calculator.

About the GED® Science Test

The GED® Science Test assesses knowledge and skills across three content areas: life science, physical science, and Earth and space science, with a breakdown of approximately 40% focusing on life science, 40% focusing on physical science, and 20% focusing on Earth and space science. Questions within these three content areas pertain to one of two main themes: Human Health and Living Systems, and Energy and Related Systems. The test uses different item types including multiple choice, short answer, fill-in-the-blank, fill-in-the-blank/short answer combination, drag-and-drop, and hotspot. All of the item types may use text passages, graphs, tables, maps, diagrams, or other information presented visually.

The GED® Science Test assesses across the Webb's Depth of Knowledge spectrum, asking students to answer questions that range from recall questions (DOK 1) to strategic thinking questions (DOK 3). The test assesses approximately 20% of its items at the DOK 1 level (recall), and 80% of its items at the DOK 2 (application of concepts) and DOK 3 (strategic thinking) levels.

On test day, you will be allowed to use the calculator provided onscreen for certain items. You will also be given an erasable note board to write out work by hand. You will not be allowed to bring your own calculator or scrap paper.

Item Types

The GED® Science Test consists of a variety of question types, multiple choice, short answer, fill-in-the-blank, fill-in-the-blank/short answer combination, drag-and-drop, and hotspot. To prepare you for the GED® Test, the Science Exercise Book models those computer-based question types in a print format to help familiarize you with what you will experience on test day.

Multiple Choice Items

The multiple-choice question is the most common type of question you will encounter. Each multiple-choice question will contain 4 answer choices, of which there will be only one correct answer. When encountering a multiple-choice question, look for any possible answers that cannot be correct based on the information given. You may also see extraneous information in the question that is used in the answer choices. Identify and eliminate this information so you can focus on the relevant information to answer the question.

> **5.** Which phenomenon on Earth would change if Earth started spinning more slowly on its axis?
>
> A. A year would be shorter.
>
> B. Seasons would not exist.
>
> C. A day would last longer.
>
> D. Eclipses would not occur.

Fill-in-the-blank (FIB) Items

A fill-in-the-blank item has you either complete a sentence by typing in a specific number, word, or phrase that completes the sentence, or typing in a specific number, word, or phrase that answers a question. If the blank occurs within a sentence, make sure to not only fill in the blank, but to make sure the sentence makes sense, keeping track of verb tenses when writing text and using appropriate units when writing numbers. Within this book, these items are simulated by writing the answer in the blank to complete the sentence.

> **4.** Ferns, redwoods, and orchids are all examples of plants classified as _____ _____.

Short Answer Items

Short answer items require a written response that is a paragraph in length. These items may ask you to explain your ideas in response to scientific information or data presented in a text passage, chart, table, diagram, or other graphic. You may find it useful to use the erasable note board that is provided to jot down notes and develop an outline before you begin to type your response to short answer items.

> **2.** In a small forest ecosystem, could you find two species of lizards living in the same population? Why or why not?
>
> _____
> _____
> _____
> _____

Fill-in-the-blank (FIB)/Short Answer Combination Items

Just as it sounds, this item type is a combination of a fill-in-the-blank item with a short answer item. You will need to type a specific number, word, or phrase that completes the fill-in-the-blank component of the item. Then, you will complete a short answer response that may require a brief paragraph.

11. In _____ transport, carrier proteins are needed to move materials across the cell membrane. Explain the reason for this phenomenon.

_____

_____

_____

_____

_____

Drop-down Items

The drop-down items are questions that give a drop-down menu within the text with choices to fill in the space to complete the sentence. There can be multiple drop-down items in a text, each with its own set of possible answers. Drop-down items are similar to fill-in-the-blank items but provide a set of possible answer choices. When answering drop-down items, try to eliminate answer choices that are meant as a distraction, including choices with unnecessary information from the text or choices that reuse information from a previous drop-down item. Within this book, these items are simulated by showing an expanded drop-down menu of multiple-choice items from which the correct answer can be selected.

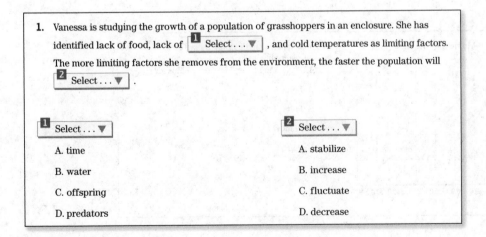

1. Vanessa is studying the growth of a population of grasshoppers in an enclosure. She has identified lack of food, lack of [**1** Select . . . ▼], and cold temperatures as limiting factors. The more limiting factors she removes from the environment, the faster the population will [**2** Select . . . ▼].

[**1** Select . . . ▼]

A. time

B. water

C. offspring

D. predators

[**2** Select . . . ▼]

A. stabilize

B. increase

C. fluctuate

D. decrease

Drag-and-drop Items

A drag-and-drop activity is an item type where you are required to drag text or images and drop them in a specific place. Examples of drag-and-drop items include sorting or classifying examples, labeling images, or sequencing parts of a process. For a drag-and-drop item, you will be given multiple items that need to be dragged, called draggables. Each draggable will need to be classified, categorized, or matched to the appropriate location, or target. Within this book, these items are simulated through writing each draggable in the appropriate target area.

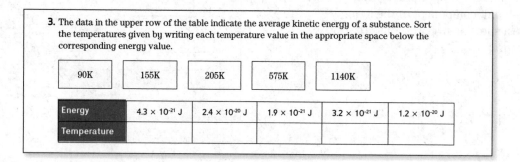

3. The data in the upper row of the table indicate the average kinetic energy of a substance. Sort the temperatures given by writing each temperature value in the appropriate space below the corresponding energy value.

90K 155K 205K 575K 1140K

Energy	4.3×10^{-21} J	2.4×10^{-20} J	1.9×10^{-21} J	3.2×10^{-21} J	1.2×10^{-20} J
Temperature					

Hotspot Items

A hotspot item consists of an image in which there are interactive spots on a graph or another image. For example, you might be asked to identify a particular part of a diagram, such as a portion of the water cycle or of a cell. This item type can also be used to plot points on graphs, number lines, and dot plots. When engaged with a hotspot item, carefully consider what the directions are asking you to do and then use the interactive image to plot points accordingly to the prompt. Within this book, these items are simulated by circling the correct portion of an image or by selecting the correct point or region from four multiple choice answer options.

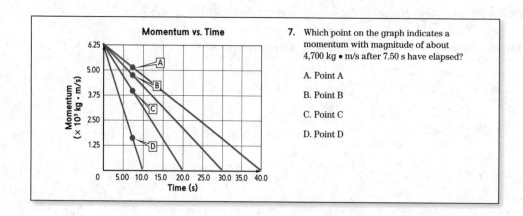

7. Which point on the graph indicates a momentum with magnitude of about 4,700 kg • m/s after 7.50 s have elapsed?

A. Point A

B. Point B

C. Point C

D. Point D

Strategies for Test Day

There are many things you should do to prepare for test day, including studying. Other ways to prepare you for the day of the test include preparing physically, arriving early, and recognizing certain strategies to help you succeed during the test. Some of these strategies are listed below.

- **Prepare physically.** Make sure you are rested both physically and mentally the day of the test. Eating a well-balanced meal will also help you concentrate while taking the test. Staying stress-free as much as possible on the day of the test will make you more likely to stayed focused.

- **Arrive early.** Arrive at the testing center at least 30 minutes before the beginning of the test. Give yourself enough time to get seated and situated in the room. Keep in mind that some testing centers will not admit you if you are late.

- **Think positively.** Studies have shown that a positive attitude can help with success, although studying helps even more.

- **Relax during the test.** Stretching and deep breathing can help you relax and refocus. Try doing this a few times during the test, especially if you feel frustrated, anxious, or confused.

- **Read the test directions carefully.** Make sure you understand what the directions are asking you to do and complete the activity appropriately. If you have any questions about the test, or how to answer a specific item type using the computer, ask before the beginning of the test.

- **Know the time limit for each test.** The Science portion of the test has a time limit of 90 minutes (1 hour 30 minutes). Try to work at a manageable pace. If you have extra time, go back to check your answers and finish any questions you might have skipped.

- **Have a strategy for answering questions.** For each question, read through the question prompt, identifying the important information to answer the question. If you need to, reread the information provided as well as any answer choices provided.

- **Don't spend a lot of time on difficult questions.** If you are unable to answer a question or are not confident in your answer, you can click on *Flag for Review* in the test window to mark the question and move on to the next question. Answer easier questions first. At the end of the test, you will be able to answer and review flagged questions, if time permits.

- **Answer every question on the test.** If you do not know the answer, make your best guess. You will lose points leaving questions unanswered, but making a guess could possibly help you gain points.

Good luck with your studies, and remember: you are here because you have chosen to achieve important and exciting new goals for yourself. Every time you begin working within the materials, keep in mind that the skills you develop in *Common Core Achieve: Mastering Essential Test Readiness Skills* are not just important for passing the GED© Test, they are keys to lifelong success.

This lesson will help you practice working with concepts related to human body systems. Use it with core lesson 1.1 Skeletal, Muscular, and Nervous Systems to reinforce and apply your knowledge.

Key Concept

The skeletal, muscular, and nervous systems work together to allow your body to react to the sights, sounds, tastes, odors, and physical contact that you encounter daily.

Core Skills & Practices

* Integrate Content Presented in Different Ways
* Determine Central Ideas

The Skeletal System

Bones provide structure to your body and protect your internal organs.

Directions: Answer the questions below.

1. Which statement gives the best example of evidence that bones are living tissue?

   A. Bones are made of calcium.

   B. A broken bone can grow back together again.

   C. Some joints are immovable while others allow a wide range of motion.

   D. Bones work together with muscles to allow body movements.

2. Bone-marrow transplants can help people who have leukemia or other blood cancers. Using what you know about bone marrow, explain why a bone-marrow transplant might help a patient with these conditions.

   _____

   _____

   _____

   _____

3. A woman has joint pain in one of her knees. Which of the following is the most likely cause of that pain?

   A. cartilage damage

   B. a semi mobile joint

   C. lack of bone marrow

   D. excess calcium in the diet

4. The shoulder is an example of a ball-and-socket joint while the knee is a hinge joint. How would bone movement be different if the knee were a ball-and-socket joint instead of a hinge?

   _____

   _____

   _____

   _____

✔ Test-Taking Tip

When you have completed your response for a short-answer test item, re-read what you wrote to make sure that your idea is clearly represented. Then, reread the question. Finally, re-read your response again to make sure that you have addressed all aspects of the question in your answer. If you need to make changes, repeat this process.

The Muscular System

Muscles move your body. They also make your internal organs work.

Directions: Answer the questions below.

5. The muscular system and the skeletal system work together. Each of these systems also works with other body systems. Which word describes the main result of the skeletal system and muscular system working together?

   A. support

   B. digestion

   C. movement

   D. protection

6. What attaches skeletal muscles to bones?

   A. tendons

   B. skin cells

   C. ligaments

   D. smooth muscles

7. Which statement best explains how muscles work to move joints?

   A. Muscles work with bones to bend or straighten joints.

   B. Muscles work independently to bend or straighten joints.

   C. Muscles work in groups of three to bend or straighten joints.

   D. Muscles work in pairs to bend or straighten joints.

8. The smooth muscles of the intestines are involuntary. Could a person survive if these muscles were voluntary? Defend your answer.

   _____

   _____

   _____

   _____

   _____

9. How does the muscular system and nervous system work together?

   _____

   _____

   _____

   _____

   _____

10. Explain the relationship between joints, bones, muscles, and tendons. Then explain what might happen if a person has tendon damage.

   _____

   _____

   _____

   _____

   _____

The Nervous System

Neurons in the brain, spinal cord, and body make up your nervous system. This network of neurons controls your body's actions and functions.

Directions: Use the diagram below to answer questions 11–12.

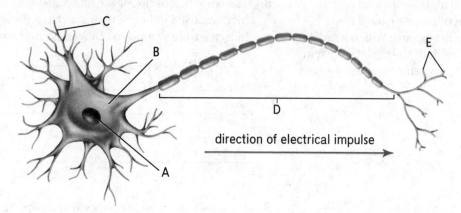

direction of electrical impulse

11. The diagram shows a neuron. What is the purpose of the neuron structure labeled D?

A. to move a nerve impulse along the neuron

B. to change electrical messages to chemical messages

C. to transfer DNA from the nucleus along the neuron

D. to carry chemical signals received from the cell body

12. Which of these correctly describes the pathway of a nerve impulse through the neuron?

A. E → D → C → B

B. A → B → C → D

C. C → B → D → E

D. E → D → A → C

Directions: Answer the questions below.

13. After a head injury, a person struggles with vision problems but does not have problems with any other senses or motor control. Which fact explains this person's experience?

A. Different parts of the brain control different body functions.

B. The brain contains 90 percent of the neurons in the body.

C. The brain's hemispheres control the opposite sides of the body.

D. The cerebellum coordinates movements of the muscles.

14. A student gathered data to compare the time it took blindfolded subjects to move their hands away from two surfaces. One surface was a cool temperature surface and the other surface was very hot. The student gathered data for 50 subjects and then calculated the average for each measurement. Which movement most likely took longer—the movement away from the cool surface or the very hot surface? Explain your answer.

_____

_____

_____

_____

This lesson will help you practice working with concepts related to human body systems. Use it with core lesson 1.2 Digestive, Excretory, Respiratory, and Circulatory Systems to reinforce and apply your knowledge.

Key Concept

The digestive, excretory, respiratory, and circulatory systems work together to move oxygen and nutrients through and out of your body.

Core Skills & Practices

- Evaluate Validity of Conclusions
- Interpret Text or Graphics

The Digestive System

Within the digestive system, ingested food is broken down through digestion, nutrients are absorbed, and wastes are eliminated.

Directions: Answer the questions below.

1. People who suffer from gallstones often have their gallbladders removed. Which of the following foods might these individuals have the most trouble digesting?

   A. a large salad

   B. a chicken breast

   C. several dinner rolls

   D. slices of pepperoni pizza

2. A researcher wants to evaluate the effectiveness of a potential weight loss medication. Which site in the digestive system is most likely to be manipulated in the study?

   A. stomach

   B. esophagus

   C. small intestine

   D. large intestine

3. Human digestion takes place along a specific pathway and follows a sequence of events. Write the correct answers in each box to show the pathway in which digestion occurs in the body.

large intestine	mouth	rectum
small intestine	stomach	esophagus

BEGINNING							END

Test-Taking Tip

When completing drag-and-drop questions that require you to sequence events, or put them in order, first verify the order requested to avoid completing the sequence in reverse. If you are unsure of all placements, begin with those you know. When you have filled in the sequence, read back over it to be sure it is logical.

The Excretory System

The excretory system is the system that removes liquid, solid, and gas wastes from the body.

Directions: Use the diagram below to answer questions 4–5.

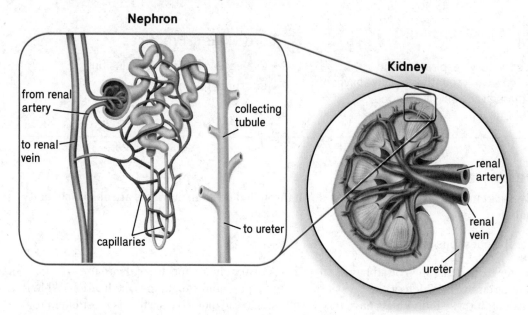

Nephron

4. Which principle of human body systems does this illustration best represent?

   A. the interaction of the circulatory and excretory systems in waste removal

   B. the role of the kidney in urine storage

   C. the necessary release of wastes in many different forms

   D. the importance of digestion for effective kidney function

5. Which characteristic of nephrons is most important to kidney function?

   A. their ability to process solid waste

   B. their total number within a kidney

   C. their detachment from capillaries

   D. their large size relative to the entire kidney

The Respiratory System

Through the respiratory system, the oxygen required for cellular respiration enters the body and carbon dioxide is released.

Directions: Answer the questions below.

6. What important lung process or structure is likely to be affected at high altitudes, where air pressures are lower?

   A. transport of blood to lungs

   B. number of working alveoli

   C. diffusion of blood to nephrons

   D. diffusion of oxygen into lungs

7. Alveoli are most similar in function and structure to which body system component?

   A. heart

   B. nephron

   C. pancreas

   D. esophagus

The Circulatory System

The circulatory system transports blood through the human body. Blood delivers water, nutrients, and oxygen to all cells in the body and carries wastes from those cells to the organs of the excretory system.

Directions: Answer the questions below.

8. Which of the following phrases best sums up the function of the circulatory system?

    A. energy generator

    B. support structure

    C. transport and delivery

    D. communication network

9. What is the most likely reason that being overweight puts an extra burden on the heart?

    A. The heart must pump more blood to nourish extra fat cells.

    B. An overweight person has an increased risk of developing diabetes

    C. The lungs may lack the capacity to deliver oxygen throughout the body.

    D. The heart of an overweight person tends to be smaller than average.

Directions: Use the diagram below to answer questions 10–12.

10. At which of the following locations is the level of carbon dioxide in blood the highest?

    A. aorta

    B. inferior vena cava

    C. superior vena cava

    D. left pulmonary artery

11. Label the image of the heart by writing the correct name in each box.

12. Why are some vessels a darker shade than others?

    _____

    _____

    _____

    _____

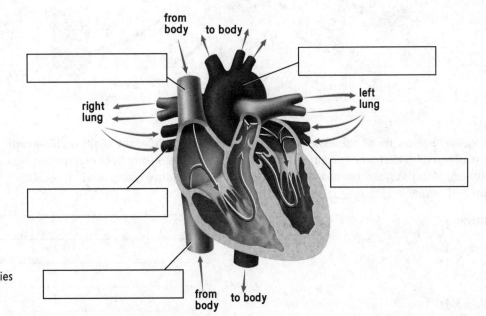

superior vena cava
inferior vena cava
aorta
right pulmonary arteries
left pulmonary veins

This lesson will help you practice working with concepts related to human body systems. Use it with core lesson 1.3 Endocrine and Reproductive Systems to reinforce and apply your knowledge.

Key Concept

The endocrine and reproductive systems are examples of body systems. Hormones in the endocrine system influence functions throughout the body, including the functions of the reproductive systems.

Core Skills & Practices

• Reconcile Multiple Findings
• Compare and Contrast Information

The Endocrine System

The endocrine system regulates many body processes through the release of hormones into the bloodstream.

Directions: Use the diagram below to answer questions 1–4.

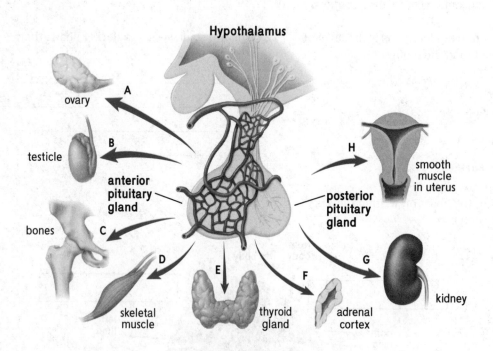

1. The diagram shows various tissues and organs that are affected by hormones produced by the pituitary gland. A rapid reaction to stress triggers a hormone in _____.

   A. pathway C

   B. pathway E

   C. pathway F

   D. pathway H

2. What does the diagram illustrate about the relationship between the hypothalamus, the pituitary gland, and target sites?

   _____
   _____
   _____
   _____
   _____

3. Which hormone pathway in the diagram is most likely to control cell growth?

A. pathway A

B. pathway C

C. pathway E

D. pathway G

4. Which statement best describes how the endocrine system triggers a response in the body?

A. Receptors on a target cell release chemicals that trigger changes in the bloodstream.

B. A nerve impulse generated in the brain travels through the bloodstream to target cells.

C. A chemical released by a gland travels through the bloodstream to target cells.

D. A chemical released by neurons travels through the bloodstream to a body organ.

The Reproductive System

The reproductive system is involved with sexual development and the production of offspring. Its functions are directed by sex hormones.

Directions: Use the diagram below to answer questions 5–7.

Female Reproductive System

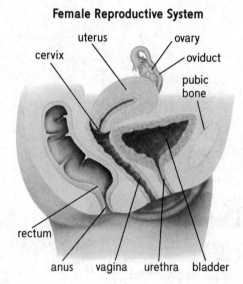

Male Reproductive System

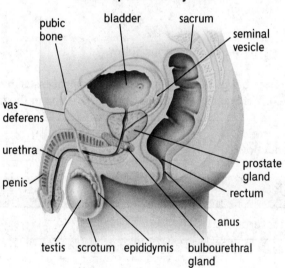

5. The structures that link the endocrine and reproductive systems are called _____.

6. Which two structures pictured carry out similar functions in females and males?

A. uterus, testes

B. uterus, male bladder

C. female bladder, scrotum

D. fallopian tube, vas deferens

7. Compare the male and female reproductive systems. Which description of reproduction is true for males but not females?

A. Gamete production is controlled by hormones.

B. Gametes mature outside the abdomen.

C. The development of gametes is cyclical.

D. The reproductive tract is separate from the bladder.

8. Which of the following is the first step in pregnancy?

A. shedding of the uterine lining

B. fertilization of the female egg

C. movement of sperm out of the scrotum

D. movement of egg through fallopian tube

9. Drinking alcohol and smoking during pregnancy can harm a developing fetus. What is the most likely reason that this is true?

A. Substances in a mother's blood cross the placenta to the fetus.

B. The mother's health is at risk throughout the pregnancy.

C. These substances could cause thinning of the uterine wall.

D. Alcohol and tobacco cause the placenta to break down.

10. During respiration, human body cells produce carbon dioxide gas as a waste product. This gas is carried to the lungs by blood and expelled during breathing. What most likely happens to the carbon dioxide gas produced by the body cells of a fetus?

A. It is reused by the fetus.

B. It stays in the mother's blood.

C. It remains in the fetus until birth

D. It is expelled by the mother's lungs.

Directions: Answer the questions below.

11. The terms below describe structures and processes involved in the endocrine control of the reproductive system. Write each term in the appropriate box in the table.

| sperm production | progesterone | estrogen | testes | thickening of uterine lining | ovary |

Hormone	Site where released	What it affects
testosterone		
		breast development
	ovary	

 Test-Taking Tip

During a test, as you are reading a question, circle or write key words that help you understand what the question is asking. For example, you might circle the words *most likely* or *best*.

This lesson will help you practice working with concepts related to regulating the body. Use it with core lesson 1.4 Homeostasis to reinforce and apply your knowledge.

Key Concept	Core Skills & Practices
Human body systems work to maintain a balanced state of internal physiological conditions even when there are changes in the external or internal environment.	• Evaluate Evidence • Express Scientific Information or Findings Visually

Homeostasis

Through homeostasis, body systems are regulated to maintain and balance the conditions needed to sustain life.

Directions: Answer the questions below.

1. Which of the following does the human body regulate to maintain homeostasis?

   A. height

   B. blood pH

   C. bone density

   D. joint mobility

2. Which of the following is least likely to be classified as an example of homeostasis?

   A. mobility in the joints

   B. cell growth in plants

   C. body temperature in animals

   D. hormone regulation in animals

3. It's a cold January day, and Veronica has forgotten her coat. Put the following stages of homeostatic response in the correct order. Write A, B, C, or D in the appropriate boxes.

   A. A signal is sent to the brain.

   B. Shivering begins, causing movement and warmth

   C. The hypothalamus signals her muscles to contract.

   D. The sensory receptors in her skin detect a change in temperature.

1	
2	
3	
4	

✓ Test-Taking Tip

Before answering a drag-and-drop question that requires you to put the answers in order, read through all of the responses and identify the first or last variable in the sequence. Place that variable in the correct position. Then determine the correct order of the other answers.

4. Which of the following is true about the relationship between a stimulus and a response?

   A. The response and the stimulus occur exactly at the same time.

   B. The stimulus always occurs before the response.

   C. The response always occurs before the stimulus.

   D. The stimulus and response are independent of each other.

5. A group of boaters has been stranded at sea for several hours. List several stimuli that would initiate a homeostatic response and identify whether each stimulus is internal or external.

_____

_____

_____

_____

_____

Directions: Use the passage below to answer questions 6–7.

The Gaia hypothesis, proposed in the 1970s by British scientist James Lovelock, states that Earth behaves as a single living organism. According to this theory, Earth regulates its own temperature, provides itself with resources needed for life, disposes of its own wastes, and fights off disease. These activities are similar to the homeostatic reactions that occur in the human body.

6. According to the passage, which of the following is evidence that Earth exhibits its own homeostatic response?

   A. Earth rotates around the sun.

   B. Other planets lack intelligent life.

   C. Earth maintains relatively constant oxygen levels.

   D. Earth supports both plant and animal life.

7. Earth exhibits a homeostatic response to a rise in temperature. For example, increased temperatures cause increased evaporation, which causes an increase in rainfall and cloud cover, cooling Earth. Explain how a parallel homeostatic response occurs in the human body in response to an increase in temperature.

_____

_____

_____

Feedback Mechanisms

Feedback mechanisms are systems set up to respond to changes in the body

Directions: Answer the questions below.

8. A puddle of water freezes when the water temperature drops below 32°F. Which statement illustrates the main difference between a puddle freezing and an animal's response to freezing temperature?

   A. An animal freezes solid at a lower temperature.

   B. An animal responds more slowly than water freezes.

   C. An animal responds in a way that best ensures its own survival.

   D. An animal does not freeze because it is not made of pure water.

9. Which of the following conditions is an example of positive feedback?

   A. increasing heart rate to raise blood pressure

   B. releasing insulin to lower blood glucose levels

   C. dilation of blood vessels to cool the body

   D. running a fever to kill pathogens in the body

Directions: Use the diagram below to answer questions 10–14.

Glucose Feedback Control

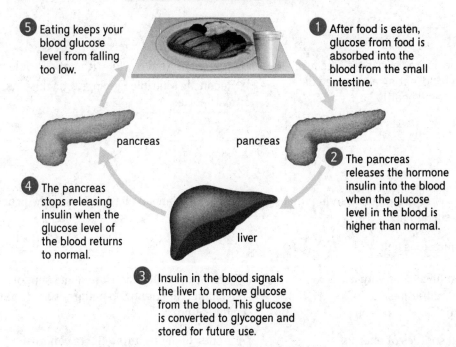

5. Eating keeps your blood glucose level from falling too low.

1. After food is eaten, glucose from food is absorbed into the blood from the small intestine.

pancreas   pancreas

4. The pancreas stops releasing insulin when the glucose level of the blood returns to normal.

2. The pancreas releases the hormone insulin into the blood when the glucose level in the blood is higher than normal.

liver

3. Insulin in the blood signals the liver to remove glucose from the blood. This glucose is converted to glycogen and stored for future use.

---

10. Which of the following can be inferred about the human body from the illustration?

A. It functions most efficiently with high levels of blood sugar.

B. It functions most efficiently with widely varying amounts of blood sugar.

C. It functions most efficiently with a limited amount of blood sugar.

D. It functions most efficiently with balanced levels of blood sugar and insulin.

11. Releasing insulin is the body's _____ to the stimulus of absorption of glucose.

12. If the body does not produce insulin, the glucose level in the blood can get dangerously _____.

13. Why is blood glucose regulation an example of a negative feedback mechanism?

A. The feedback cycle damages the body.

B. The purpose is to reverse changes in the body.

C. The purpose is to accelerate changes in the body.

D. The feedback cycle sometimes operates in reverse.

14. How might a doctor use blood glucose tests to determine if the glucose feedback control is working properly in a patient? Explain your response.

_____

_____

_____

_____

_____

This lesson will help you practice working with concepts related to eating a healthy diet rich in nutrients. Use it with core lesson 1.5 Nutrition to reinforce and apply your knowledge.

Key Concept

Your body depends on six key nutrients. Because nutrients come from food, eating a balanced diet contributes to your overall health.

Core Skills & Practices

- Represent Real World Arithmetic Problems
- Reconcile Multiple Findings, Conclusions, or Theories

Nutrients

Nutrients nourish and provide energy to all living things. Eating a well-balanced diet containing the proper nutrients is necessary to sustain life.

Directions: Answer the questions below.

1. Which statement best illustrates why a diet extremely low in carbohydrates could be considered unhealthy?

    A. Sugars are natural sources of energy.

    B. Fiber is essential for smooth digestion.

    C. Carbohydrates digest fats and proteins.

    D. Carbohydrates are the body's main source of energy.

2. Manuel does not like to eat meat but wants to begin bodybuilding. A friend advises him to consume both milk and peanut butter as sources of protein. Why would both be helpful?

    A. The body cannot digest plant-based proteins without animal-based proteins.

    B. Plant-based proteins often lack many amino acids present in animal products.

    C. Proteins work best when eaten in both a liquid and solid form.

    D. Peanut butter is not a naturally occurring source of protein but milk is.

3. Which of the following statements supports the claim that eating too many saturated fats is unhealthy?

    A. Foods high in saturated fats can raise blood cholesterol.

    B. Foods high in saturated fats usually come from animals.

    C. Foods high in unsaturated fats reduce the risk of heart disease.

    D. Foods high in saturated fats contain very few vitamins.

4. Which of the following are inorganic elements that the body needs for most of its metabolic functions?

    A. proteins

    B. minerals

    C. nutrients

    D. vitamins

Directions: Use the diagram below to answer questions 5–7.

Fat Content for Selected Products
(present in one 25-gram serving)

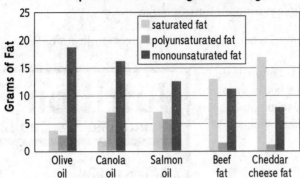

5. What information do you need to determine which of the food products in the chart is most healthful?

   A. the number of grams contained in each ounce of the food

   B. the risks and benefits of each type of fat contained in the food

   C. the presence of each type of fat in other commonly eaten foods

   D. the total number of calories allowed each day on a person's diet

6. Which products might be substituted in the diet of someone who is trying to lower cholesterol level by reducing consumption of saturated fat?

   A. beef instead of salmon

   B. canola oil instead of olive oil

   C. olive oil instead of canola oil

   D. cheddar cheese instead of beef

7. Studies have shown that polyunsaturated fats may help reduce the risk of type 2 diabetes. Which product would a doctor most likely recommend to a patient at risk for developing this disease?

   A. beef fat

   B. olive oil

   C. canola oil

   D. cheddar cheese fat

Directions: Answer the question below.

8. Fatima likes to eat only bagels, eggs, nectarines, salad, spaghetti, and yogurt. She wants to consume at least one fruit or vegetable, one carbohydrate, and one protein with each meal but does not want to repeat the same meal in one day. Design a lunch and dinner menu that meets her needs.

bagel	eggs	nectarine	salad	spaghetti	yogurt

Lunch			
Dinner			

Eating a Healthy, Balanced Diet

If your diet is balanced, that means you are eating meals that provide a variety of the nutrients the body needs. Food labels provide valuable information to help you make wise food choices. Use them to make decisions toward the most healthful choices for your nutritional needs.

Directions: Use the nutrition label below of a serving of cereal to answer questions 9–10.

9. Nutrition facts are based on percent daily values for a 2,000 calorie diet. Based on a 2,000 calorie diet, if you ate two servings with one cup milk, what percent daily value of potassium will you consume?

   A. 4%

   B. 10%

   C. 16%

   D. 20%

10. If you snacked on 2 servings of dry cereal, how many calories would you consume?

    A. 180 Calories

    B. 225 Calories

    C. 270 Calories

    D. 360 Calories

Nutrition Facts
Serving Size 3/4 Cup (27g)

Amount Per Serving	Cereal	With 1/2 Cup Skim Milk
Calories	90	130
Calories from Fat	10	10
	% Daily Value	
Total Fat 1g*	2%	2%
Saturated Fat 0g	0%	0%
Trans Fat 0g	0%	0%
Cholesterol 0mg*	0%	0%
Sodium 190mg*	8%	11%
Potassium 85mg*	2%	8%
Total Carbohydrates 23g*	8%	10%
Dietary Fiber 5g	20%	20%
Sugars 5g		
Protein 2g*		
Vitamin A	0%	4%
Vitamin C	10%	15%
Calcium	0%	15%
Iron	2%	2%

Directions: Answer the following question.

11. Humans must burn 3,500 Calories to lose one pound of fat. If Jiang burns 1,800 Calories per day but consumes only 1,550 Calories per day, it will take him _____ days to lose one pound of fat.

✓ **Test-Taking Tip**

After completing a fill-in-the-blank question, reread the entire sentence and make sure that the answer you wrote makes sense in the context of the sentence.

This lesson will help you practice working with concepts related to disease, the immune system, and disease prevention. Use it with core lesson 1.6 Disease Prevention to reinforce and apply your knowledge.

Key Concept

Disease can be caused by something introduced into the body, like a virus, or by improper care of the body. Many diseases can be prevented by taking advantage of advances in medical science and by practicing healthy behaviors.

Core Skills

• Understand and Explain a Non-textual Scientific Presentation
• Distinguish Between Cause and Effect

Disease

A disease is any condition that disrupts the normal functioning of the body. Diseases can be classified as infectious and non-infectious.

Directions: Answer the questions below.

1. Which disease is caused by a pathogen?

   A. arthritis

   B. cirrhosis

   C. diabetes

   D. hepatitis

   2. Explain how a sneeze transmits a cold from one person to another.

   _____

   _____

   _____

   _____

3. How do infectious diseases differ from non-infectious diseases?

   A. Infectious diseases may be passed genetically from parent to child, but non-infectious diseases cannot be.

   B. Infectious diseases disrupt the normal functioning of the body, while non-infectious diseases do not.

   C. Infectious diseases cannot be passed by contact with another person, but non-infectious diseases can.

   D. Infectious diseases are caused by bacteria, viruses, or parasites, while non-infectious diseases are not.

✔ Test-Taking Tip

When completing a short-answer question, read the question carefully. Make sure that your answer clearly addresses the information that is asked for.

Directions: Use the passage below to answer questions 4–5.

Many pathogens are transmitted by vectors. Vectors are animals that spread pathogens through their saliva, parasites, body waste, and meat. Some of the infectious diseases that require a vector include malaria, rabies, and bubonic plague. Bubonic plague is transmitted from infected rats to humans by fleas. This disease, also known as the Black Death, killed more than half the population of Europe during an epidemic in the fourteenth century.

4. Which disease would be transmitted by a vector?

A. cancer

B. *E. coli*

C. diabetes

D. arthritis

5. Based on the information in the passage, explain why diseases like malaria and bubonic plague are classified as infectious diseases and why they require a vector.

_____

_____

_____

_____

_____

The Immune System

The immune system is the body's defense against pathogens.

Directions: Answer the questions below.

6. Which is a defense that makes it difficult for a pathogen to invade the body?

A. B cells

B. T cells

C. bone marrow

D. mucous membranes

7. How do T cells distinguish between healthy body cells and infected cells?

A. Infected cells cause inflammation that attracts the T cells.

B. T cells produce proteins that attach to antigens on the infected cells.

C. Infected cells are marked by antibodies that the T cells recognize.

D. T cells recognize proteins located on the walls of healthy cells.

8. Order the events that occur as a pathogen invades the body through the skin. Write the appropriate letter in each box below.

A. B cells and T cells are produced

B. antigens trigger immune response

C. B cells attach antibodies to the pathogens

D. T cells destroy infected cells and pathogens marked by antibodies

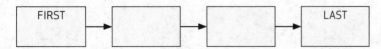

FIRST → ☐ → ☐ → LAST

Preventing Disease

In the mid-nineteenth century, scientists made the connection between germs and disease. Based on this discovery, ways of preventing the spread of disease have been developed and have saved millions of lives.

Directions: Answer the questions below.

9. Which will not help to prevent the transmission of syphilis?

   A. getting a vaccine

   B. proper condom use

   C. refraining from sex

   D. limiting sexual partners

10. Which action would be the most effective in preventing the spread of Salmonella from one food source to another?

    A. washing your hands thoroughly before handling cooked poultry

    B. covering your mouth whenever you cough

    C. cooking all food thoroughly at a very high temperature

    D. cleaning a knife used to cut poultry before using it for other food

Directions: Use the information from the table below to answer questions 11–12.

Causes of Disease before and after Vaccine Availability in the U.S.		
Disease	Average Number of Cases per Year before Vaccine Available	Cases in 1998 after Vaccine Available
measles	503,282	89
diphtheria	175,885	1
tetanus	1,314	34
mumps	1,152,209	606
rubella	47,745	345
pertussis (whooping cough)	147,271	6,279

11. According to the table, which vaccine was most effective in eradicating a disease?

    A. tetanus vaccine

    B. rubella vaccine

    C. measles vaccine

    D. diphtheria vaccine

12. Based on the information in the table, summarize the overall effectiveness of these vaccines?

    _____

    _____

    _____

    _____

This lesson will help you practice working with concepts related to interactions between living organisms and their environment. Use it with core lesson 2.1 Living Things and Their Environment to reinforce and apply your knowledge.

Key Concept

Organisms interact with the living and nonliving parts of their environment. Climate and other environmental factors influence how populations and communities develop around the world.

Core Skills & Practices

• Analyze Relationships between Sources
• Make a Prediction Based On Data or Evidence

The Living Environment

Interactions among organisms and their environment include both the living (biotic) and nonliving (abiotic) parts of the environment.

Directions: Answer the questions below.

1. What is one example of an abiotic factor in a marine environment?

   A. fish that eat algae

   B. shift in tides and its timing

   C. reproduction in microorganisms

   D. competition among sharks for food

2. In a small forest ecosystem, could you find two species of lizards living in the same population? Why or why not?

   _____

   _____

   _____

   _____

Directions: Use the passage below to answer questions 3–4.

Competition for limited resources is an important relationship among organisms in an ecosystem. For example, in a pond both bass and ducks eat small fish. The greater the number of fish eaten by ducks, the less food for the bass. Each animal has more than one source of food, so this competition is not likely to lead to any complete population starving. However, competition, mainly for food, limits the size of each population. In a stable ecosystem, each population stays about the same size. The number of each species that dies is balanced by the number of newborns that survive.

3. What would be a sign of the ecosystem becoming unstable?

   A. Environmental conditions change seasonally.

   B. The bass and ducks compete for food.

   C. The bass population grows and the duck population declines.

   D. There are abundant small fish for predators.

4. Using the description given, predict what might happen to the niches of ducks and bass if the populations of small fishes decreased.

   _____

   _____

   _____

   _____

Directions: Answer the questions below.

5. Sort the levels of ecology to match each research question. Complete the table by writing the level of ecology in the appropriate space.

| population | community | ecosystem |

Research Question	Level of Ecology Studied
How does hurricane damage in a wetland affect the food chain there?	
How do birds in a flock behave to prevent predators from taking their eggs?	
How does the addition of a bass to a pond affect the populations of other fish species?	

6. Within a coral reef, several species of fish live in the same area. Some hide among corals and filter passing plankton, others actively chase and eat smaller fish, and still others nibble on the coral itself. Based on this evidence of these species' differences, what do you predict is the main cause of these various "occupations" represented in the coral reef ecosystem?

A. how food resources can be limited

B. how population sizes can be affected

C. how adaptations help determine niches

D. how environmental conditions cause crowding

Biomes

Biomes are large regions defined by climate characteristics and contain similar organisms adapted to those conditions.

Directions: Answer the questions below.

7. A still, shallow pond supports cattails and grasses at its edge, and fishes, frogs, and insects within. A sunlit coral reef includes algae, fishes, crabs, and corals. What do these two freshwater and marine biomes have in common?

A. Each supports plant life.

B. Each is affected by tides.

C. Both are primarily low-oxygen environments.

D. Both support life only at the surface.

8. Biomes vary in the types and numbers of organisms that they support. Some biomes have environmental conditions that are more severe than others, sustaining only organisms particularly adapted to those conditions, whereas other biomes have environmental conditions that are "hospitable" enough to sustain a variety of organisms. Which two biomes support similar levels of biological diversity?

A. desert and coral reef

B. shallow pond and deep ocean

C. tundra and tropical rain forest

D. tropical rain forest and coral reef

Directions: Use the diagram to answer questions 9–11.

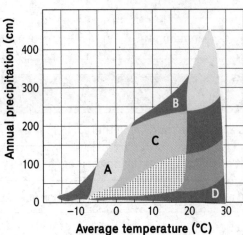

Annual Precipitation v. Temperature for Various Biomes

9. The labeled biome that is both coldest and driest is _____.

10. Based on the diagram and your general knowledge of biomes, predict which list correctly orders four land biomes from driest to wettest.

   A. tundra→deciduous forest →desert →grassland

   B. tundra→ grassland→ deciduous forest→temperate rain forest

   C. desert→temperate rain forest→tropical rain forest→deciduous forest

   D. temperate rain forest→grassland→tundra →tropical rain forest

11. Which region of the diagram represents a desert biome?

   A. Region A

   B. Region B

   C. Region C

   D. Region D

Test-Taking Tip

In a computer-based test environment, you may be asked to click on a region of a graph to select the correct answer. When completing these types of hot spot questions, keep in mind that the location of the identified point in the diagram or graph is critical to your answer choice. To narrow down your range of answers, first determine what makes that spot different from other locations on the figure. Eliminate answers that would obviously not meet these criteria.

This lesson will help you practice working with concepts related to how organisms move energy and matter through ecosystems. Use it with core lesson 2.2 Movement of Energy and Matter to reinforce and apply your knowledge.

Key Concept

Organisms move energy and matter through ecosystems. Energy is lost as it passes through a community of organisms, but matter is recycled and used over and over again.

Core Skills & Practices

- Identify and Refine Hypotheses for Scientific Investigations
- Analyze Relationships Among Terms

Energy Flow in an Ecosystem

Energy is conserved as it moves through an ecosystem: Energy changes in form as some is absorbed by organisms and some is released as heat.

Directions: Answer the questions below.

1. Which statement correctly describes all producers in any food web?

   A. Producers require the Sun's energy to produce organic molecules.

   B. Producers provide energy for all other organisms in a food web, except decomposers.

   C. Producers are a direct source of organic compounds for herbivores and omnivores.

   D. Producers make up the smallest organisms in the food web.

2. How do decomposers link the flow of energy in an ecosystem to the cycling of matter?

   A. Decomposers cause other organisms to lose energy in the form of heat.

   B. Decomposers limit the contribution of nutrients from other organisms.

   C. Decomposers produce oxygen when they break down other organisms.

   D. Decomposers release nutrients from dead organisms into the environment.

Directions: Use the food chain diagram below to answer questions 3–4.

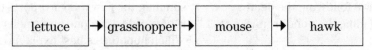

lettuce → grasshopper → mouse → hawk

3. Which organism shown is a first-order heterotroph?

   A. hawk

   B. mouse

   C. lettuce

   D. grasshopper

4. What might a food web tell you about this community of organisms that this food chain does not? Provide specific examples in your answer.

   _____

   _____

   _____

Directions: Use the passage below to answer questions 5–6.

At the turn of the century, ranchers moved onto the grassy Kaibab Plateau in northern Arizona. They were attracted by the fine grazing areas and large numbers of deer for hunting. Fearing that the mountain lion, another inhabitant of the region, would prey on the cattle and deer, the ranchers waged a campaign to eliminate the cat from the plateau. They were successful in their efforts, and mountain lions disappeared within a few years. However, the success of the ranchers at eliminating mountain lions produced terrible ecological results. Increased numbers of deer, along with herds of grazing cattle, stripped the land of all grasses. Soon, heavy rains caused major erosion, and the land was reduced to a fraction of its usefulness. This problem has occurred repeatedly where humans have changed an ecosystem without considering the possible consequences.

5. What did the ranchers do that initially disrupted the food web in the Kaibab Plateau ecosystem?

A. reduced the population of secondary consumers

B. brought in cattle, stimulating producers

C. upended the energy pyramid by hunting omnivores

D. eliminated habitat needed by autotrophs

6. How can the effects on the Kaibab Plateau ecosystem be described in terms of components of the food web?

A. Autotrophs increased, which increased heterotrophs.

B. Second-order heterotrophs decreased, which increased first-order heterotrophs.

C. First-order heterotrophs decreased, which decreased second-order heterotrophs.

D. First-order heterotrophs decreased, which decreased autotrophs.

Cycles of Matter

Water and nutrients are constantly recycled within ecosystems as they move through various biogeochemical cycles.

Directions: Answer the questions below.

7. Students participating in a biology field course are attempting to measure and graph the oxygen cycle in a local pond ecosystem over time. What change might they observe following the deaths of half the plants surrounding the pond from a fungal disease?

A. a sudden release of oxygen to the atmosphere

B. a decline in oxygen released to the atmosphere

C. an increase in oxygen buried as organic matter

D. an increase in carbon dioxide produced by heterotrophs

8. During one spring, the local newspaper reports that a flock of Canada geese has settled and is raising goslings at the pond in a town park. That summer, the newspaper reports that the pond is covered with algae and smells like dead fish. Which hypothesis best explains the connection between these two events?

A. The geese disrupted the water cycle by decreasing runoff.

B. The geese avoided algae as a food source.

C. The geese contributed excessive carbon to the carbon cycle.

D. The geese contributed nitrogen that caused eutrophication in the pond.

Directions: Use the diagram below to answer question 9.

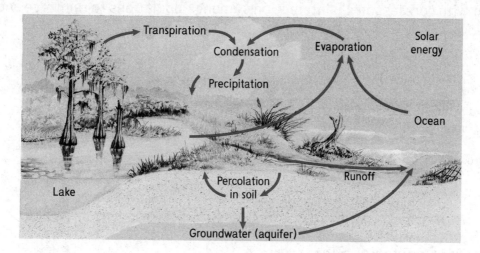

9. A developer receives permits allowing him to cut down the trees in the pictured swamp and fill in part of the lake. Using the table below, sort out how these changes might directly alter the cycling of matter in this ecosystem. Complete the table by writing the affected process next to the correct effect of the alteration.

Effect of ecosystem alteration	Process affected
Loss of trees	
Loss of lake	
Decrease in percolation	
Decrease in evaporation	

Decreased groundwater	Decreased runoff
Decreased transpiration	Decreased condensation

![checkmark] **Test-Taking Tip**

During an exam, it often helps to take a momentary break, shut your eyes, and take a few deep breaths. It will help you clear your head and stay fresh during the exam session. Just two or three 30-second breaks can be very beneficial.

This lesson will help you practice working with concepts related to interactions among populations. Use it with core lesson 2.3 Interactions Among Populations to reinforce and apply your knowledge.

Key Concept

Many factors control the growth of a population in an area. The maximum size of a population that a specific environment can sustain over time can be influenced by interactions among populations.

Core Skills & Practices

- Describe a Data Set Statistically
- Evaluate Reasoning

Factors that Affect Population Size

Limiting factors reduce the growth rate of a population.

Directions: Read the passage below. Then choose the option that correctly completes each sentence.

1. Vanessa is studying the growth of a population of grasshoppers in an enclosure. She has identified lack of food, lack of **1** Select . . . ▼ , and cold temperatures as limiting factors. The more limiting factors she removes from the environment, the faster the population will **2** Select . . . ▼ .

1 Select . . . ▼

- A. time
- B. water
- C. offspring
- D. predators

2 Select . . . ▼

- A. stabilize
- B. increase
- C. fluctuate
- D. decrease

✓ Test-Taking Tip

When answering a drop-down question, try to read the passage and think of the answer on your own before looking at the answer choices. This will help you quickly eliminate answer choices that do not fit the context of the passage.

Directions: Answer the questions below.

2. Cougars are known predators of deer. Relatively soon after cougar hunting was legalized, the deer population in Sherman Forest spiked. A decade later scientists noted the deer population was declining due to widespread starvation. In this scenario, _____ became a limiting factor. Explain why.

_____

_____

_____

3. Mikhela has been tracking the moose population in a state park. According to the following figures, the estimated carrying capacity for this stable moose population in the park is _____.

	Year 35	Year 36	Year 37	Year 38	Year 39
Moose population	138	152	145	144	145

Directions: Use the graph below to answer questions 4–6.

Trout Population in a Lake

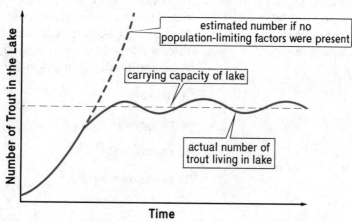

4. After the carrying capacity is reached, what will be true about the trout population in the lake?

   A. The average number of trout will remain stable over time.

   B. The average number of trout will slowly increase over time.

   C. The average number of trout will slowly decrease over time.

   D. The average number of trout will remain stable but for only a short time.

5. Which of the following would least likely be classified as a population-limiting factor for the trout?

   A. water pollution in the lake

   B. the presence of other species in the lake that feed on trout eggs

   C. bacteria in the lake that cause diseases in fish

   D. the presence of many insect species along the shore of the lake

6. Which of the following can you infer to be true about the trout population if there were no population-limiting factors?

   A. It would slowly decrease over time.

   B. It would remain relatively stable over time.

   C. It would show an exponential increase over time.

   D. It would reach a threshold and then result in extinction.

Lesson 2.3 Interactions Among Populations

Symbiosis

A close relationship between individuals of two or more species is called symbiosis.

Directions: Use the passage below to answer questions 7–8.

When animals and plants live together in the same environment, such as a forest or a lake, special nutritional relationships develop among many of the different organisms. In a predator-prey relationship, one organism kills and eats a second organism. In a parasitic relationship, one organism takes nutrients from the living body of another organism and in doing so may harm but does not immediately kill the other organism. In a mutualistic relationship, organisms form relationships that benefit all of the organisms. In a commensal relationship, one organism benefits from a second organism while the second organism neither benefits nor is harmed.

7. As uninvited guests, small beetles often live in the nest of an ant colony, helping themselves to food supplies built up by the ants. During a season when food resources are plentiful, the portion of food taken by the beetles is not missed. How would you classify this relationship?

   A. parasitic

   B. mutualistic

   C. commensal

   D. predator-prey

8. A fungus causes the disease chestnut blight in the American chestnut tree. This fungus takes nutrients from the tree and damages plant tissue on any part of the tree on which it grows. Eventually, chestnut trees usually die from this disease. How do you classify the relationship of the chestnut-blight fungus to the chestnut tree?

   A. parasitic

   B. mutualistic

   C. commensal

   D. predator-prey

Predator-Prey Relationships

Predation is a type of symbiosis where one organism kills and eats another organism.

Directions: Answer the questions below.

9. A biologist tracking the population of hawks and mice has noted that as the population of hawks increased, the population of mice tapered off and began to decline. What is the most likely cause for this decrease?

   A. The growing hawk population is increasingly killing more mice.

   B. The mice population has contracted a disease and is dying off.

   C. The ecosystem has become polluted and both populations will decline.

   D. The food sources for mice are decreasing at an exponential rate.

10. Camouflage is a widely seen method in nature by which an organism blends into its background environment. An organism may exhibit both the color and shape characteristics of its surroundings. Which of the following types of organisms stands to benefit **most** from camouflage?

   A. prey

   B. host

   C. parasite

   D. pollinator

This lesson will help you practice working with concepts related to disruptions to ecosystems and the consequences or impact of these disruptions. Use it with core lesson 2.4 Disruptions to Ecosystems to reinforce and apply your knowledge.

Key Concept	Core Skills & Practices
Ecosystems can be disrupted by both natural events and human activities. Disruptions can have a significant impact on organisms and the entire ecosystem.	• Reason From Data or Evidence to a Conclusion • Distinguish Among Reasoned Judgments

Natural Disruptions to Ecosystems

Natural hazards that disrupt ecosystems include volcanic eruptions, wildfires, and flooding.

Directions: Use the passage below to answer questions 1–2.

On the morning of May 18, 1980, an earthquake under Mount St. Helens started a tremendous volcanic eruption. The north face of the mountain slid away in a huge avalanche, releasing a blast of superheated, rock-filled gas that ripped up the trees in its path. By the afternoon, slower, hotter flows of gas and rock had destroyed the trees and killed all living organisms in the soil. Mature forests were turned into ash-covered wasteland.

Since then, hardy plants have reappeared in the ash field. The plants attract herbivores that drop seeds from other plants in their dung. More than three decades after the eruption, the forest is beginning to regrow.

1. How were new plants introduced into the ecosystem of Mount St. Helens after the volcanic eruption?

   A. through wind-blown seeds

   B. in the ash of burned vegetation

   C. by animals returning to the area

   D. with the flows of heated gas and rock

2. As used in the passage above, the word avalanche means a(n) _____ .

   A. lava flow

   B. explosion

   C. large snow slide

   D. massive rock slide

Directions: Answer the question below.

3. Areas along a river that experience regular flooding are called floodplains. Why might floodplains be productive land for growing crops?

   A. Flooding can improve the pH balance of the water used to irrigate crops.

   B. Flooding can provide a healthy layer of standing water to enrich the soil.

   C. Flooding can clear the land of animals and invasive plants that threaten crops.

   D. Flooding can enrich depleted soil by depositing a layer of nutrient-rich sediment.

Human Effects on Ecosystems

Modern humans can impact the natural world significantly through habitat destruction and increased pollution. These effects of human activity alter ecosystems, contribute to global warming, and threaten sensitive species with extinction.

Directions: Use the information below to answer questions 4–6.

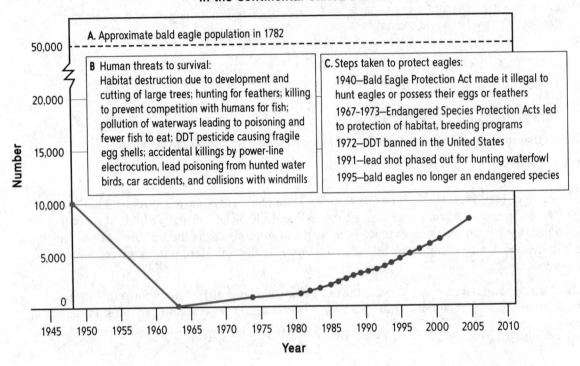

Nesting Pairs of Bald Eagles in the Continental United States

A. Approximate bald eagle population in 1782

B Human threats to survival:
Habitat destruction due to development and cutting of large trees; hunting for feathers; killing to prevent competition with humans for fish; pollution of waterways leading to poisoning and fewer fish to eat; DDT pesticide causing fragile egg shells; accidental killings by power-line electrocution, lead poisoning from hunted water birds, car accidents, and collisions with windmills

C. Steps taken to protect eagles:
1940–Bald Eagle Protection Act made it illegal to hunt eagles or possess their eggs or feathers
1967-1973–Endangered Species Protection Acts led to protection of habitat, breeding programs
1972–DDT banned in the United States
1991–lead shot phased out for hunting waterfowl
1995–bald eagles no longer an endangered species

4. The bald eagle is a large bird of prey that lives near water in every U.S. state except Hawaii. Based on the graph above, why was lead shot phased out in 1991?

   A. Hunters using lead shot would often mistake eagles for waterfowl.

   B. Lead shots that missed waterfowl were hitting eagles instead.

   C. Lead shot was polluting the waterways used by eagles and waterfowl.

   D. Eagles were being poisoned from eating waterfowl killed with lead shot.

5. Based on the evidence above, form a conclusion about how the ban on DDT appears to have affected bald eagle populations.

   _____

   _____

   _____

6. Which sequence best describes the link between fossil fuels and the loss of habitats along ocean shorelines?

   A. rise in global temperatures → burning of fossil fuels → release of carbon dioxide into the atmosphere → melting of polar ice caps → rise in sea levels

   B. burning of fossil fuels →release of carbon dioxide into the atmosphere → rise in global temperatures → melting of polar ice caps → rise in sea levels

   C. release of carbon dioxide into the atmosphere → rise in sea levels → melting of polar ice caps → burning of fossil fuels → rise in global temperatures

   D. burning of fossil fuels → melting of polar ice caps → rise in sea levels → release of carbon dioxide into the atmosphere → rise in global temperatures

Directions: Answer the questions below.

7. Why have human biological control efforts often been unsuccessful?

   A. Natural enemies destroy the newly introduced organism in the new environment.

   B. People have not understood how the change will affect the entire ecosystem.

   C. The newly introduced organism has been unable to adapt to the environment.

   D. People have misidentified the problem that they are trying to solve

8. Which statement best explains how overhunting harms ecosystems?

   A. It weakens one species and permits the introduction of another, which may negatively affect the ecosystem.

   B. The removal of one species from an ecosystem causes changes in the food web and disrupts the entire ecosystem.

   C. When one animal is removed, it becomes necessary to find a replacement that will return balance to the ecosystem.

   D. By reducing a particular animal population, it endangers a valuable source of food and other materials required by humans.

Directions: Use the passage below to answer questions 9–11.

> Wolves were reintroduced to Yellowstone National Park in 1995. Through hunting, wolves cut the elk population in half. With fewer elk, more cottonwood and aspen trees grew. The trees fed beaver and provided homes for birds. By controlling the number of elk, the wolves made the forest more diverse.

9. Explain the meaning of "biodiversity." Then explain how the elk were affecting the biodiversity within Yellowstone National Park before the wolves were reintroduced.

   _____

   _____

   _____

   _____

   _____

   _____

10. According to the passage, wolves _____ the biodiversity of Yellowstone National Park.

11. Based on information in the passage, which statement is most likely true?

    A. Reintroducing wolves to Yellowstone National Park may restore a healthy equilibrium to the ecosystem.

    B. Removing the wolves from Yellowstone National Park brought about beneficial changes to the ecosystem.

    C. The biodiversity within the park will continue to increase as wolves further reduce the elk population.

    D. The natural balance between organisms and their environment will prevent the wolves within the park from over-populating.

✓ Test-Taking Tip

When completing a multiple choice question on a test, it is generally best to go with your first answer selection. When a person changes an answer, the changed answer is often not correct.

This lesson will help you practice working with concepts related to cells. Use it with core lesson 3.1 Cells: Basic Units of Life to reinforce and apply your knowledge

Key Concept

Your tissues, organs, and body systems all have one thing in common—they are composed of cells. Cells are the basic units of structure and organization of all living organisms.

Core Skills & Practices

- Understand and Apply Scientific Models, Theories, and Processes
- Analyze Author's Purpose

Cell Discovery and Cell Theory

Cells are the smallest living units that carry on the activities of an organism.

Directions: Use the passage below to answer questions 1–3.

> The discovery of the microscope in the seventeenth century helped lead scientists away from the theory of spontaneous generation. With careful experimentation, scientists discovered that even microbes such as bacteria could be killed by boiling, and once killed they did not lead to new life forms.
>
> The death of the theory of spontaneous generation led to the work of the French biologist Louis Pasteur. Pasteur showed that if matter was sterilized and prevented from being contaminated, then bacteria and other microscopic life forms did not arise on their own. The same principle can be shown by the sterilization of hospital instruments, which keeps the instruments bacteria free and prevents the spread of harmful diseases.

1. Which statement best summarizes the author's purpose in this passage?

    A. To describe the debate between two equally supported scientific views

    B. To show the process by which the theory of spontaneous generation was rejected

    C. To explain why Louise Pasteur is regarded as one of the most important scientists of the 19th century

    D. To explore the importance of the discovery of the microscope

2. Which of the following best defines the concept of spontaneous generation as used in the passage?

    A. a belief that living things come from nonliving matter

    B. the theory that contaminated matter can become uncontaminated

    C. the idea that energy can neither be created nor destroyed

    D. a notion that microscopic life forms did not arise on their own

3. How does the author use the sterilization of hospital instruments to disprove the theory of spontaneous generation?

    _____

    _____

    _____

Directions: Use the passage and diagram below to answer questions 4–6.

Italian physician Francesco Redi proposed that maggots did not suddenly appear out of nowhere on rotting meat. Instead, he believed that maggots came from eggs laid by flies that land on the meat. To test his hypothesis, he set out jars: some were open to air and some were covered with cheesecloth. Air can pass through cheesecloth, but flies cannot.

Control Group

Experimental Group

4. Label the variables in Redi's experiment as independent or dependent.

Variable	Type
Time	
Cheesecloth	
Maggots	

5. Which of the following does the evidence from Redi's experiment serve to disprove?

A. cell theory

B. pasteurization

C. cell specialization

D. spontaneous generation

6. Why did Redi choose to use air-permeable cheesecloth for the experiment?

A. to show that air carries bacteria that can spoil meat

B. to allow the flies to lay eggs into the jar but not land on the meat

C. to show that maggots are not microscopic organisms floating in the air

D. to prove that air, not flies, causes the growth of maggots in unrefrigerated meat

 Test-Taking Tip

When answering a multiple-choice test question, try to answer the question in your own words or generate a hypothetical answer first. Then use your answer to help eliminate answer choices that do not follow similar logic.

Specialized Cells and Cellular Organization

Different cells are equipped to do specific jobs.

Directions: Answer the questions below.

7. What type of tissue is mainly involved in carrying impulses to the brain?

A. muscle

B. nerve

C. epithelial

D. connective

8. Rank the following in order from the most basic to the most complex parts of the body.

A. cells

B. organs

C. tissues

D. body systems

1.

2.

3.

4.

9. Cells must maintain enough surface area to absorb the materials needed for metabolism. They can grow only so large before their surface area is too small compared to their volume. What is the underlying assumption behind this need for a small surface-area-to-volume ratio?

A. Large cells have more efficient metabolic reactions.

B. Small cells have more efficient metabolic reactions.

C. Small cells have more metabolic reactions to fuel than large cells.

D. Large cells have more metabolic reactions to fuel than small cells.

10. What type of tissue is the responsible for forming linings and coverings for body parts?

A. muscle

B. nerve

C. epithelial

D. connective

11. Blood is considered a type of _____ tissue.

12. Blood consists of red blood cells, which carry oxygen; white blood cells, which fight disease; and platelets, which assist with clotting. Explain the purpose of this type of specialization.

_____

_____

_____

_____

13. Each type of tissue listed in the box below contributes to the functioning of the human digestive system. Write the letter of the function in the box with the corresponding tissue type.

A. Allows the body to swallow food

B. Lines the stomach and digestive tract

C. Signals the body to begin the digestive process

D. Generates contractions to move the food along the digestive trac

Tissue type	Function
Connective	
Epithelial	
Muscle	
Nervous	

This lesson will help you practice working with concepts related to cell structure and function. Use it with core lesson 3.2 Cell Structure and Function to reinforce and apply your knowledge.

Key Concept

Animal and plant cells have many of the same cell parts. The parts of a cell help the cell carry out the functions of life.

Core Skills

• Determine the Meaning of Symbols, Terms, and Phrases
• Make Inferences

The Parts of a Cell

Different jobs are performed by structures within the cell called organelles.

Directions: Answer the questions below.

1. What is the function of the cell membrane?

   A. control center for the cell

   B. regulator of traffic passing into and out of the cell

   C. manufacturer of proteins from amino acids

   D. means of transportation for material within the cell

2. Which structure within the cell of an orange most likely holds the orange juice?

   A. vacuole

   B. ribosome

   C. lysosome

   D. Golgi apparatus

3. Label the parts of the cell. Write the appropriate term in each box.

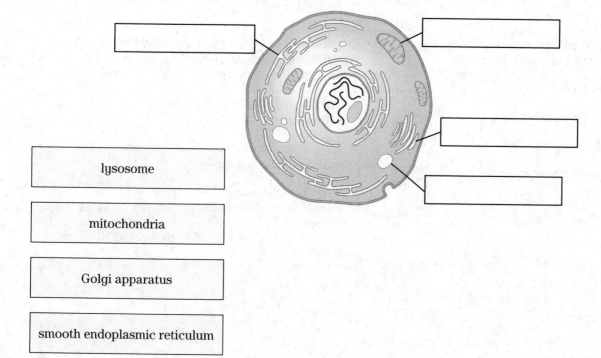

lysosome

mitochondria

Golgi apparatus

smooth endoplasmic reticulum

Distinguishing Between Cells

Directions: Answer the questions below.

4. Mushrooms, like other fungi, do not use energy from the sun to produce glucose. Instead, they obtain their nutrients by absorbing them from other living or dead organisms. Knowing this, which cell structure would likely be absent from a mushroom cell?

   A. nucleus

   B. cell wall

   C. cytoplasm

   D. chloroplast

5. Unlike prokaryotic cells, _____ cells have a nucleus and organelles enclosed by membranes.

6. Which cell structure makes a raw carrot crunchy to eat?

   A. vacuole

   B. cell wall

   C. chloroplast

   D. mitochondria

7. Which structure is found in plant cells but not in animal cells?

   A. nucleus

   B. cell wall

   C. cytoplasm

   D. cell membrane

Directions: Use the passage below to answer questions 8–9.

There is a type of single-celled organism called prokaryotes. Prokaryotes are organisms in which the cells do not contain a nucleus or any other specialized cell structures. Bacteria and mildew are examples. However, although bacterial cells do not contain a nucleus, they do contain genetic material. Bacteria reproduce by a process called binary fission. During binary fission, a bacteria cell divides into two identical cells, each cell receiving one copy of the genetic material.

8. According to the passage, what makes prokaryotes unlike most other plant cells?

   A. the absence of a nucleus

   B. the absence of a cell wall

   C. their smaller than normal size

   D. the presence of genetic material

9. In eukaryotic cells, genetic information is contained in a nucleus. How might this impact the way they reproduce?

   A. They would only be able to create cells without nuclei.

   B. They would be able to reproduce more quickly than prokaryotes.

   C. They would require a carrier protein to release their genetic information.

   D. They would not be able to reproduce using binary fission.

Transport Across the Cell Membrane

Cell membranes are selectively permeable. Some substances can move through cell membranes whereas others cannot.

Directions: Answer the questions below.

10. How does the process of diffusion function in the human body?

A. It is initiated in times of extreme illness and stress.

B. It regulates blood flow between organs through veins and arteries.

C. It concentrates materials, where needed in the body, through stockpiling.

D. It allows certain substances to pass into and out of cells without using energy.

11. In _____ transport, carrier proteins are needed to move materials across the cell membrane. Explain the reason for this phenomenon.

_____

_____

_____

_____

_____

✓ Test-Taking Tip

When answering a combination fill-in-the-blank and short-answer question, first identify the words that could plausibly fill in the blank. Take a moment to consider how each one would affect the answer you would give for the short-answer part of the question. Choose the answer that best completes the sentence and provides a logical foundation for the short-answer portion.

Directions: Use the passage below to answer questions 12–13.

A cell's cytoplasm contains many substances in varying degrees of concentration. These concentrations differ sharply from those in the fluid surrounding the cell. Such differences are so essential that the cell can die if the differences are not maintained. Given the opportunity, diffusion would quickly eliminate these critical differences by moving the substance from an area of high concentration to an area of lower concentration. Therefore, the cell must be able to negate, and sometimes even reverse, the process of diffusion.

12. Which of the following best describes the meaning of **diffusion** in this passage?

A. the passage of light through the fluid surrounding the cell

B. the maintenance of differences in concentration across a cell membrane

C. the softening of the cell membrane to allow for active transport

D. the movement of a substance from an area of high to low concentration

13. Which is a way in which cells reverse the process of diffusion?

A. by using the Golgi apparatus to manufacture hormones

B. by using the endoplasmic reticulum to move molecules through the cell

C. by using carrier proteins to push materials back across the cell membrane

D. by using mitochondria to generate more energy

This lesson will help you practice working with concepts related to plant varieties and the parts of plants essential to their growth and survival. Use it with core lesson 3.3 Plant Structure and Function to reinforce and apply your knowledge.

Key Concept	Core Skills & Practices
The parts of a plant work together to promote and sustain the life of the plant. The functions of the plant structures provide mechanisms for all of the plant's life processes.	• Design a Scientific Investigation • Analyze Relationships Between Sources

Types of Plants

Plants provide people with essential materials for physical comfort while adding beauty to their lives. Most plants can be classified as flowering or non-flowering.

Directions: Answer the questions below.

1. Which types of plant require a wet environment for their survival?

   A. mosses

   B. seed plants

   C. angiosperms

   D. gymnosperms

2. Junipers are cone-bearing evergreens with needle-like or scale-like leaves. In which plant group does the juniper belong?

   A. seedless

   B. angiosperms

   C. gymnosperms

   D. nonvascular plants

3. A student wants to perform an investigation to find out how young plants respond to the movement of a light source. Which of these is the dependent variable for this scientific investigation?

   A. age of plants

   B. amount of light

   C. height of plants

   D. plant movement

4. Ferns, redwoods, and orchids are all examples of plants classified as _____ _____.

5. Describe two similarities and two differences between gymnosperms and angiosperms.

   _____

   _____

   _____

6. The maple tree fruit is a two-sided winged fruit. A student wants to study the dispersal range of the maple tree seeds. When designing the investigation, which question would yield the most relevant data?

   A. How much sunlight will the seeds receive daily?

   B. Has flood or fire recently disrupted the ecosystem?

   C. How will the seeds interact with freezing temperatures?

   D. How does the wind interact with the plant traits?

Directions: Use the passage below to answer questions 7–8.

Osmosis

Most cell membranes are selectively permeable membranes, which means that some particles can pass across them while others cannot. Perhaps the most important substance that passes through the cell membrane is water. Water molecules pass through a selectively permeable membrane by a type of diffusion known as osmosis. During osmosis, water molecules move from a place of higher concentration of water to a place of lower concentration of water—either into or out of the cell.

When there is a difference in the concentration of a solution outside a cell compared with the material inside the cell, osmosis will occur. If the concentration of solute particles outside the cell is higher than the concentration inside the cell material, water diffuses out of the cell, causing the cell to shrivel. If the concentration of solute particles inside the cell material is higher than the concentration outside the cell, water diffuses into the cell. This causes the cell to swell.

7. Explain how osmosis relates to water absorption and use by non-vascular plants.

_____

_____

_____

8. Predict what will most likely occur with nonvascular plants during hot, dry weather.

A. They will lose water from their cells.

B. They will halt the process of diffusion.

C. They will slow the process of diffusion.

D. They will store extra water in their cells.

Parts of Plants

Plants have various parts that support the essential functions of life. Cells, tissues, and organs work together to ensure the growth and survival of the plant.

Directions: Answer the question below.

9. Summarize the life cycle of an angiosperm by writing the steps in this process in the correct order in the boxes below.

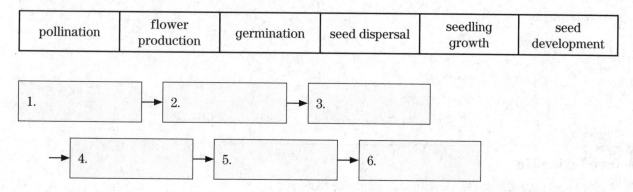

pollination	flower production	germination	seed dispersal	seedling growth	seed development

1. → 2. → 3.

→ 4. → 5. → 6.

10. Which is an example of an "organic molecule" produced by photosynthesis?

A. oxygen gas

B. chloroplast

C. carbohydrate

D. carbon dioxide gas

11. In which part of a plant would unused energy most likely be stored?

A. the xylem

B. the taproot

C. the stomata

D. the epidermis

Directions: Use the illustration below to answer questions 12–13.

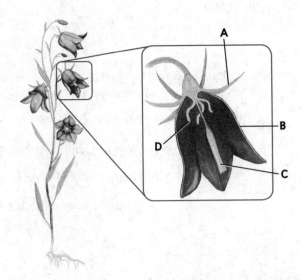

12. What is an important function of the flower part labeled A?

A. to catch sunlight

B. to aid pollination

C. to store nutrients

D. to protect the bud

13. Study the lettered areas of the illustration. In which part of the flower are pollen grains produced?

A. Part A

B. Part B

C. Part C

D. Part D

 Test-Taking Tip

Some hot spot items may ask you to identify a structure or region on a diagram. On a computer-based test, you would answer the question by clicking on the correct structure or region. Evaluate the diagram and eliminate the hot spots you know are incorrect before selecting your answer.

This lesson will help you practice working with concepts related to energy and cells. Use it with core lesson 3.4 Energy and Cells to reinforce and apply your knowledge

Key Concept

Plant cells use energy from the Sun to make sugars. Plant and animal cells break down sugars and other food molecules to release energy that cells can use.

Core Skills & Practices

- Express Scientific Information Symbolically
- Distinguish between Facts and Speculation

Photosynthesis

The process by which organisms capture light energy from the Sun and change it into chemical energy is called photosynthesis.

Directions: Use the diagram below to answer questions 1–3.

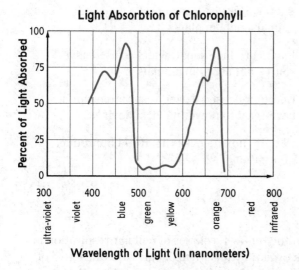

Light Absorbtion of Chlorophyll

Percent of Light Absorbed

Wavelength of Light (in nanometers)

1. During the process of photosynthesis, which two colors of light are absorbed most by chlorophyll?

   A. blue and green

   B. blue and orange

   C. green and yellow

   D. violet and yellow

2. Which of the following is an example of a speculative statement based on this graph?

   A. The color of chlorophyll is greenish-yellow.

   B. Chlorophyll that absorbs blue light is a product of evolution.

   C. Photosynthesis relies on energy from the Sun.

   D. Chlorophyll absorbs more blue light than green light.

3. Light that is not absorbed by chlorophyll is reflected off the plant, giving it its color. Which of the following would be least likely to have a light-absorption graph similar to the graph above?

   A. ferns

   B. broccoli

   C. lawn grass

   D. mushrooms

Cellular Respiration

Plants, animals, and other organisms release the energy stored in the organic molecules of food through cellular respiration.

Directions: Use the passage below to answer questions 4–5.

> The proper balance of carbon dioxide and oxygen gases in the atmosphere is needed for life to be possible on Earth. The carbon-oxygen cycle relies on two processes: cellular respiration and photosynthesis.
>
> During cellular respiration, cells in a plant or animal use oxygen to break down sugar and release energy. Carbon dioxide gas is a byproduct.
>
> Photosynthesis is the process in which plants take in carbon dioxide from the atmosphere. During photosynthesis, plant cells using sunlight as an energy source combine carbon dioxide gas and water to produce sugar. Oxygen gas is given off as a byproduct.

4. Which definition best matches the use of the word **photosynthesis** as used in the passage?

   A. The process of absorbing oxygen gas and changing it into chemical energy.

   B. The process of capturing light energy and changing it into chemical energy.

   C. The process of capturing light energy and using it to release chemical energy.

   D. The process of absorbing oxygen gas and using it to release chemical energy.

5. Which of the following is an example of a speculative statement?

   A. Photosynthesis does not take place in animals, only in plants.

   B. Plants produce sugar, which is used as a source of energy in animals.

   C. Energy released during respiration can be harnessed to power medical devices.

   D. Carbon dioxide gas is a natural byproduct of breathing.

Directions: Answer the questions below.

6. Most of the process of cellular respiration occurs in the organelles known as _____. Explain why the enzymes in these organelles are necessary for the process of energy transformation.

   _____

   _____

   _____

   _____

7. Put the following stages of cellular respiration in the order in which they occur. Write the letter of the process in the space provided in the boxes.

   A. glycolysis

   B. Krebs cycle

   C. oxidative phosphorylation

   D. transformation of pyruvate

Stages of Cellular Respiration

Fermentation

When cells cannot get the oxygen they need, they use a process called fermentation to release the energy stored in organic molecules.

Directions: Use the information below to answer questions 8–9.

The chemical equation for the fermentation of alcohol is as follows:

$$C_6H_{12}O_6 \rightarrow 2C_2H_5OH + 2CO_2 + heat$$

8. Which of the following best describes the chemical process shown above?

    A. aerobic because oxygen is required

    B. anaerobic because carbon dioxide is not required

    C. anaerobic because oxygen is not required

    D. aerobic because carbon dioxide is required

9. Cells use fermentation to release stored energy when oxygen is not available. Using the equation shown, explain why fermentation is useful in such a situation.

_____

_____

_____

_____

 Test-Taking Tip

Before answering a short answer question, rule out what the question is **not** asking. Then, organize your thoughts around what you do know about the topic. After you have written your answer, check back over the question to be sure you followed all directions accurately.

Directions: Answer the questions below.

10. How does the energy yield from fermentation compare to the energy yield from cellular respiration?

    A. Fermentation yields less energy than cellular respiration.

    B. Fermentation yields more energy than cellular respiration.

    C. Fermentation yields energy that is only usable by animals.

    D. Fermentation yields energy that is only usable by plants.

11. Which of the following products does **not** rely on the process of fermentation for its manufacture?

    A. butter

    B. cheese

    C. yogurt

    D. alcohol

12. During lactic acid fermentation, which of the following is converted into lactic acid?

    A. ATP

    B. glucose

    C. pyruvate

    D. acetyl coenzyme A

This lesson will help you practice working with concepts related to mitosis and meiosis. Use it with core lesson 3.5 Mitosis and Meiosis to reinforce and apply your knowledge.

Key Concept

Cells divide through the process of mitosis or meiosis. Mitosis produces daughter cells that are identical to the parent cell. Meiosis produces sex cells that combine to produce offspring that are genetically different from parent cells.

Core Skills & Practices

- Analyze Events and Ideas
- Understand and Explain Non-Textual Scientific Presentations

Cell Growth and Division

The process by which one parent cell divides into two daughter cells is known as cell division, or cell reproduction.

Directions: Answer the questions below.

1. Prokaryotes reproduce through binary fission, while _____ undergo a process known as the cell cycle. What is the reason for the difference in the methods of cell division used by each group of organisms?

   _____

   _____

   _____

   _____

2. Which of the following characterizes both of the gap phases of the cell cycle?

   A. cell growth

   B. cell division

   C. nuclear division

   D. DNA replication

3. During interphase, cells increase in size and their DNA is copied. What is the purpose of this stage of the cell cycle?

   A. to prepare the cell for division

   B. to protect the cell against pathogens

   C. to reduce the number of chromosomes by half

   D. to restore normal functioning after division

4. Several stages of the cell cycle are listed. Put the stages of the cell cycle in order from first to last (cell division) by writing the letter of the phase in the appropriate box.

   A. mitosis

   B. synthesis

   C. Gap 1 (G$_1$)

   D. Gap 2 (G$_2$)

   E. cytokinesis

First
Last

 Test-Taking Tip

When answering a drag-and-drop sequencing question, begin by identifying the first or last item in the sequence. If you do not know the first or last item in the sequence, start with two items that you know are adjacent to each other in the sequence.

Chromosomes and Cell Division

Chromosomes are made up of DNA wrapped with proteins and can contain thousands of genes.

Directions: Use the diagram below to answer questions 5–6.

Four Stages of Mitosis

prophase   metaphase   anaphase   telophase

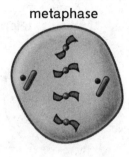 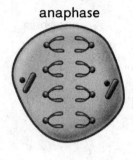 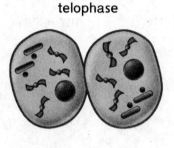

5. Which part of the cell is the main focus of the diagram?

   A. nucleus

   B. chromosomes

   C. cell membrane

   D. nuclear membrane

6. During which stage do sister chromatids move to opposite ends of the cell?

   A. prophase

   B. anaphase

   C. telophase

   D. metaphase

Directions: Use the passage below to answer questions 7–8.

Sometimes, exposure to radiation and certain kinds of chemicals can cause an error when a cell duplicates its chromosomes before mitosis. This error results in a change in a gene that is passed on to new cells. A change in the genes or chromosomes of a cell is called a mutation. Some mutations are minor and have no visible effect. Other mutations, however, are major and cause loss of function or other harm to the organism. Inherited mutations cause such conditions as muscular dystrophy, hemophilia, and sickle-cell anemia.

7. Which of the following summarizes the main idea of this passage?

   A. Mutations are destructive to cells.

   B. Mutations are inherited changes to the chromosomes.

   C. Cell replication can sometimes result in mutations.

   D. Radiation and chemicals can make mitosis impossible.

8. Based on the passage, what is the relationship between genes and chromosomes?

   A. Chromosomes are the determinants of the severity of a genetic mutation.

   B. Chromosomes are the proteins responsible for activating genes.

   C. Chromosomes are the structures on which genes are located.

   D. Chromosomes are responsible for initiating mutations in genes.

Sexual Reproduction

Sexual reproduction involves meiosis, a form of cell division in which the nucleus divides twice to reduce the number of chromosomes by half.

Directions: Use the diagram below to answer questions 9–10.

Four Stages of Meiosis

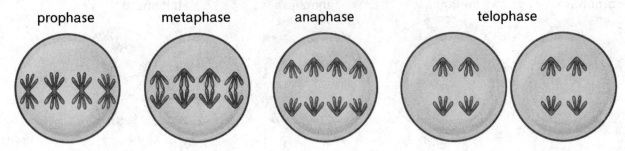

prophase   metaphase   anaphase   telophase

9. During which stage are two nuclei created?

A. prophase

B. anaphase

C. telophase

D. metaphase

10. The end result of meiosis is four gametes or reproductive cells. Explain what occurs after the final stage shown in the diagram in order to accomplish this end. How do the cells at the end of this process differ from those shown in the final stage represented in the diagram?

_____

_____

_____

_____

Directions: Answer the questions below.

11. Which of the following best describes the purpose of meiosis II?

A. to split sister chromatids

B. to unite two different sex cells

C. to prepare the nucleus for replication

D. to separate homologous chromosomes

12 The protein structures responsible for pulling apart the chromosomes during cell division are known as _____ fibers.

13. All of the cells in the human body contain 46 chromosomes except for the _____, which cannot carry the same number of chromosomes as those of other parts of the body.

14. How does the division of gametes differ from the division of zygote cells?

A. Gametes divide by mitosis; zygote cells divide by meiosis.

B. Gametes divide by meiosis; zygote cells divide by mitosis.

C. Gametes divide by meiosis; zygote cells divide by binary fission.

D. Gametes divide by binary fission; zygote cells divide by meiosis.

This lesson will help you practice working with concepts related to the basic principles of genetics. Use it with core lesson 4.1 Basic Principles of Genetics to reinforce and apply your knowledge.

Key Concept

Some characteristics of organisms are passed from parents to offspring. How this occurs and characteristics of offspring can be studied on the molecular level.

Core Skills & Practices

• Describe a Data Set Statistically
• Apply Scientific Processes

Traits, Heredity, and Genetics

Traits are passed from parents to offspring. This passing of traits from one generation to the next is known as heredity. The field of biology devoted to studying heredity is called genetics..

Directions: Use the table below to answer questions 1–3.

Consider a trait in a desert lizard species that is controlled by two alleles, one dominant and one recessive. The table below shows the percentages of lizards that have the dominant trait in three lizard populations.

Lizard Population	Population Size	Percentage of the Population with the Dominant Trait
A	120	30
B	90	20
C	100	40

1. What percentage of population B has the recessive trait?

   A. 20   C. 80

   B. 40   D. 90

2. Based on the data in this table, what can you infer about dominant traits in a population?

   A. Dominant traits are usually the most common type of trait in a population.

   B. Dominant traits are not always the most common type of trait in a population.

   C. Dominant traits are almost never the most common type of trait in a population.

   D. Dominant traits are almost always the most common type of trait in a population.

3. Population _____ has the greatest number of individuals with the dominant trait. In this population, there are _____ individuals with the dominant trait.

✓ Test-Taking Tip

Before answering a question that asks you to refer to a data, check that you understand what the numbers represent in each cell of the table. When reading the relevant question, be careful to direct your attention to the appropriate spot in the table. If answer choices are provided, check each against the data presented. When you select an answer, read the question and the data table again to check that you have interpreted the question correctly.

Chromosomes, Genes, and Alleles

Genes, which are found within chromosomes, are segments of DNA that determine traits; different forms of a gene are called alleles.

Directions: Use the illustration below to answer questions 4–5.

	Seed Shape	Flower Color	Pod Color	Plant Height
Dominant Trait	round W	purple P	green G	tall T
Recessive Trait	wrinkled w	white p	yellow g	short t

4. Sort the allele combinations to match each set of traits exhibited in Mendel's pea plants. Complete the table by writing the allele combination in the appropriate space.

GGPPTtWw		GgppTTWW		ggPpttww

Traits Exhibited	Allele Combination
tall plant with white flowers, round seeds, and green pods	
tall plant with purple flowers, round seeds, and green pods	
short plant with purple flowers, wrinkled seeds, and yellow pods	

5. Why is it that the expression of most traits that organisms exhibit cannot be accurately represented in this type of illustration?

   A. Most traits are determined by more than one gene.

   B. Most traits are not clearly defined as dominant or recessive.

   C. Most traits are determined by single alleles, not a combination.

   D. Most traits do not depend on the contribution of particular alleles.

Directions: Answer the questions below.

6. Which statement accurately describes a component of chromosome replication?

   A. Sister chromatids are not identical.

   B. Sister chromatids are present only after replication.

   C. Homologous chromosomes are identical.

   D. Homologous chromosomes do not replicate.

7. What are the interacting roles played by DNA, genes, chromosomes, and alleles in determining heredity?

   _____

   _____

   _____

   _____

Inheritance and Meiosis

The patterns of inheritance described by Gregor Mendel can be explained by the cellular process of meiosis, which produces gametes—egg and sperm.

Directions: Answer the following questions.

8. A cell cannot function properly if it has too few or too many 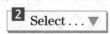 . Sexual reproduction, then, must involve a form of cell division in which the nucleus divides in a way that is different from 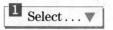 . Gametes are produced during a type of cell division that involves meiosis. Cell division that involves meiosis occurs only in the production of male gametes (sperm) and female gametes (eggs).

1 Select . . . ▼

A. alleles

B. nuclei

C. gametes

D. chromosomes

2 Select . . . ▼

A. meiosis

B. mitosis

C. replication

D. fertilization

9. Which process would involve the production of gametes?

    A. rapid growth in a bamboo plant

    B. splitting of single-celled amoeba

    C. development of a fetus from a zygote

    D. pollination and fertilization in a pine tree

10. Why doesn't a zygote formed through fertilization have twice as many chromosomes as its contributing parents?

    A. Gametes divide during meiosis.

    B. Each chromosome replicates after meiosis.

    C. The number of parent chromosomes is halved during meiosis.

    D. Homologous chromosome pairs separate, joining sister chromatids.

11. Which allele combination could be found in gametes produced by a parent organism with the allele combination of DdrrAACc?

    A. DdAC

    B. DrAc

    C. DrrAC

    D. DdrrAACc

This lesson will help you practice working with concepts related to determining the probability of inherited traits in organisms. Use it with core lesson 4.2 Probability of Traits to reinforce and apply your knowledge.

Key Concept

Some traits are inherited. The probability of inheriting a trait can be calculated.

Core Skills & Practices

- Use Percents
- Determine the Probability of Events

Inheriting Traits

The traits of an organism are determined by the alleles, or forms of a gene, that it inherits from its parents.

Directions: Answer the questions below.

1. In pea plants, yellow seeds (Y) are dominant and green seeds (y) are recessive. If a pea plant has green seeds, what combination of alleles make up its genotype?

    A. YY only

    B. yy only

    C. Yy only

    D. YY or yy

2. Which alleles could be used to represent an organism that is heterozygous for a trait?

    A. p

    B. PP

    C. Pp

    D. pp

3. The phenotype of an organism describes its _____. How does phenotype differ from the genotype of the organism? Give an example to support your answer.

    _____

    _____

    _____

    _____

 Test-Taking Tip

A short-answer test question may have two or more parts. When answering a short-answer question that has more than one part, separate the parts of the question. As you write your answer, mentally check off each part to ensure that you provide a complete answer.

Punnett Squares

A Punnett square shows how alleles for traits can combine during a cross of two parents to produce specific genotypes and phenotypes in the offspring.

Directions: Answer the question below.

4. In cats, the curled ear allele (C) is a dominant trait expressed by ears that are curled backwards. Cats that express this gene appear to have normal ears for the first three or four months of life, then their ears begin to curl backwards. The allele for standard ears in cats (c) is recessive. Suppose a cross between two curled-ear cats, each with the genotype Cc, produces four kittens. What will a Punnett square reveal about the potential phenotype for each kitten?

   A. All kittens will have curled ears.

   B. Each kitten has a 25% chance of having curled ears.

   C. Each kitten has a 50% chance of having curled ears.

   D. Each kitten has a 75% chance of having curled ears.

5. In pea plants, yellow seeds (Y) are dominant over green seeds (y). Complete the Punnett square shown to show the possible genotype outcomes of a cross between a pea plant that is heterozygous for yellow seeds and homozygous for green seeds.

Predicting Traits

Punnett squares help you use traits of the parents to predict the combinations of alleles that produce traits in offspring.

Use the diagram below to answer questions 6–8.

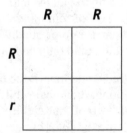

8. In the diagram shown, *R* represents round seeds and *r* represents wrinkled seeds. Based on this information, the probability that an offspring from this cross will have wrinkled seeds is

   _____ .

6. The Punnett square shows a cross between two organisms where round (R) seeds are dominant. Complete the Punnett square to show the possible genotype outcomes. Write your answers in the appropriate box.

7. Based upon the information provided in the Punnett square above, what percentage of offspring do you predict will have round seeds? Of these, what percentage do you predict will be homozygous for this trait? Explain your answer.

   _____

   _____

   _____

   _____

Multiple Traits and Other Patterns of Heredity

Punnett squares can be used to find the probability of multiple traits, traits that are determined by genes carried by sex chromosomes, and traits that have multiple alleles.

Directions: Answer the questions below.

9. Which of the following is an example of a trait that is determined by multiple alleles?

   A. height in pea plants

   B. gender determination

   C. blood groups in humans

   D. flower color in pea plants

10. In humans, what combination of chromosomes results in a male child?

    A. XY

    B. XX

    C. YY

    D. XXX

11. What is the probability of a trait that is predicted for 2 out of 16 offspring?

_____

_____

Directions: Use the diagram below to answer questions 12–14.

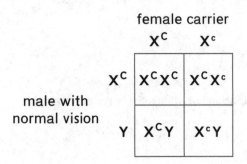

12. The Punnett square above shows the outcomes of a genetic cross between a male with normal color vision and a female carrier for red-green color blindness. What is the probability of the couple producing a daughter who is a carrier for colorblindness?

    A. 0%

    B. 25%

    C. 50%

    D. 100%

13. The designation _____ in the Punnett square indicates that color blindness is a sex-linked trait carried on the X chromosome.

14. Hairy ears are inherited as a Y-linked trait. Suppose a man with hairy ears (XY^A) marries a woman without hairy ears (XX). Which statement correctly describes how the resulting genotype pattern for hairy ears will compare to the genotype pattern for color blindness illustrated in the Punnett square?

    A. One of four children could inherit the gene for hairy ears, but only the male child would be affected. Two of four children could inherit the gene for color blindness, but the affected child could only be female.

    B. Two of four children could inherit the gene for hairy ears, but only the female children would be affected. Two of four children could inherit the gene for color blindness, but the affected child could only be male.

    C. One of four children could inherit the gene for hairy ears, but the only a female child would be affected. Two of four children could inherit the gene for color blindness, and the affected children could be male or female.

    D. Two of four children could inherit the gene for hairy ears, but only the male children would be affected. Two of four children could inherit the gene for color blindness, and the affected children would be male.

This lesson will help you practice working with concepts related to evolution, including theories and methods of study that support and explain common ancestry and biological evolution. Use it with core lesson 4.3 Common Ancestry to reinforce and apply your knowledge.

Key Concept

The Theory of Universal Common Ancestry suggests that all organisms on Earth evolved from a single common ancestor. Scientists construct diagrams and charts to show how seemingly diverse species share common traits.

Core Skills & Practices

- Make Inferences
- Evaluate Whether a Conclusion or Theory is Supported or Challenged by Particular Data or Evidence

Darwin and Evolution

English naturalist Charles Darwin proposed a theory of evolution which holds that all forms of life developed over time from different and often much simpler ancestral organisms.

Directions: Use the passage to answer questions 1–2.

To understand the significance of a fossil and to recognize the conditions in which the organism lived, a scientist needs to know the age of the fossil. Scientists can use the order of the layers of sedimentary rock to estimate the age of any fossils in the rock. Because lower layers of rock are older than upper layers, a fossil in a lower layer must be older than a fossil in an upper layer.

Three of the four eras of geological time are documented in the walls of North America's Grand Canyon. There are nearly 40 identified rock layers forming the canyon walls. Coral fossils have been found in the limestone caprock, on the rim of the Grand Canyon. Fossils of trilobites, extinct marine animals with hard outer skeletons, have been found deep in the canyon in slopes cut by erosion.

1. Which statement is likely true?

   A. Trilobites are older than corals.

   B. Corals and trilobites share a common ancestry.

   C. Corals and trilobites are the same age.

   D. Trilobites are more advanced than corals.

2. What aspect of Darwin's theory of evolution does the absence of trilobite fossils in higher rock layers support?

   A. Life on Earth has changed over time, and some organisms have died out.

   B. Organisms with soft bodies or thin shells will rarely form fossils.

   C. Living things will adapt over time to better survive their environment.

   D. Isolated organisms may develop traits not apparent in the original population.

The Theory of Universal Common Ancestry

In addition to the theory of evolution, Darwin proposed that all organisms that have ever lived on Earth descended from a single primitive ancestor. This is known as the theory of Universal Common Ancestry (UCA).

Directions: Answer the following questions.

3. A great white shark and a mako shark share a common ancestor. Because they are different [1] Select... ▼ , however, they cannot [2] Select... ▼ and produce fertile [3] Select... ▼ .

[1] Select... ▼

A. species

B. animals

C. individuals

[2] Select... ▼

A. compete

B. interbreed

C. live in freshwater

[3] Select... ▼

A. species

B. gametes

C. offspring

4. Biologists have discovered that the DNA of human beings is very similar to the DNA of many other animals, such as mice and chimpanzees. How does this information relate to the theory of UCA?

A. It supports the theory that genetics play a key role in evolution and that a single organism can produce species that do not look alike.

B. It suggests that the organisms share a genetic link to a common biological ancestor, which may support the theory of UCA.

C. It implies that humans are not related to other organisms such as plants and bacteria and thus contradicts the theory of UCA.

D. It confirms that seemingly unrelated species can develop from one species that lived in the past, which supports the theory of UCA.

5. Based on the ideas proposed by UCA, what is the connection between adaptation and biodiversity?

_____
_____
_____
_____
_____
_____
_____
_____

Cladograms

Scientists can study the relationship of organisms using cladistics, a method of describing evolutionary relationships between species using diagrams called cladograms, which are similar to a family tree

Directions: Answer the following questions.

6. Scientists have used cladograms to explore the theory of universal common ancestry. What has been the result?

    A. By diagramming the evolutionary relationships between species, scientists have traced the origins of each species back to a single common ancestor.

    B. By examining the evolutionary development of each species, scientists have learned there is no link between the three domains of life.

    C. By diagramming the adaptive traits of living organisms, scientists have deduced that each species has evolved over time.

    D. By examining the physical traits of living organisms, scientists have discovered organisms that do not share a common ancestor.

7. On a cladogram, a cow has more structural traits in common with a whale than a frog. What can be inferred from this information?

    A. The cow and the whale have the same common ancestors as the frog.

    B. The cow and the whale are more closely related than the cow and the frog.

    C. The cow and the whale have evolved over time, while the frog has not.

    D. The cow and the whale are closer to the universal common ancestor than the frog.

8. The steps for constructing a cladogram are described in the boxes below. Put the steps for constructing a cladogram in their correct sequence. Write each step in the appropriate box.

A. List or draw each organism.	B. Choose structural traits to compare.	C. Draw circles around the species that share a trait.
D. Choose the species you would like to compare.	E. Make a table matching organisms and traits.	F. Use this information to construct a cladogram.

Step 1	Step 2	Step 3	Step 4	Step 5	Step 6

 Test-Taking Tip

In a computer-based test, sequencing questions such as the one above may require that you drag and drop answers into the correct box. Decide how to sequence your answers before you begin. If possible, decide on the first and last items in the sequence. This will make the remaining items easier to arrange.

This lesson will help you practice working with concepts related to heredity, sources of heritable genetic variation, and environmental influences on genetic expression. Use it with core lesson 4.4 Heredity: Genetic Variations and Expression to reinforce and apply your knowledge.

Key Concept

Offspring from sexual reproduction have a unique set of traits. There are various causes of changes in traits from one generation to the next.

Core Skills & Practices

- Make Predictions Based upon Data or Evidence
- Cite Textual Evidence

Genetic Variation

The variation in human and animal species can be traced back to genes, the expressions of genes, and the interaction of genes and the environment.

Directions: Use the illustration below to answer questions 1–2.

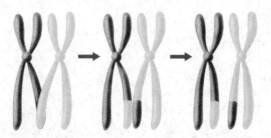

1. Which process does the illustration best demonstrate?

   A. It demonstrates how strands of a DNA molecule separate during replication.

   B. It demonstrates why mutations can be passed from parent to child.

   C. It demonstrates why a child can show a mixture of family characteristics.

   D. It demonstrates how an error may occur in the genetic material of a cell.

2. Which statement about the illustrated process its true?

   A. It occurs only in male gametes.

   B. It occurs during an early phase of mitosis.

   C. It allows the redistribution of linked genes.

   D. It results in reduced genetic variation among gametes.

 Test-Taking Tip

When answering a multiple choice question, cover the answer options and read the question stem. Try to answer the question on your own. Next, read the stem with each option and eliminate the options you know are incorrect. Finally, select the answer that seems to most closely answer the question.

Directions: Answer the questions below.

3. A cut on your hand heals as the result of
_____ .

   A. DNA replication

   B. genetic recombination

   C. electromagnetic radiation

   D. mutation of a single allele

4. Which is not a characteristic of a mutation?

   A. creates a permanent change in DNA

   B. is a failure of the replication process

   C. may compromise an organism's fitness

   D. allows healthy diversity among organisms

5. Genetic errors can occur during replication or other normal processes related to genetic material. Categorize these results of genetic error by writing them in the correct column of the table below. One item will be used twice.

| cancer | Down Syndrome | cystic fibrosis |

| May be passed on, parent to child | Cannot be passed on, parent to child |

Genetic Information Lost (switched or added at the chromosome level)	Error in DNA Coding within Egg or Sperm Cells	Errors During Replication that affect Body Cells

Directions: Choose the correct terms to complete the sentences below.

6. When an organism reproduces, new traits may occur that benefit the offspring. These traits are the result of the process called 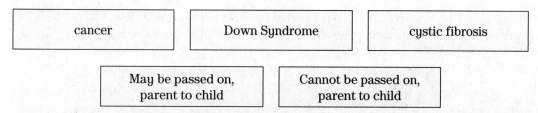 **1** Select . . . ▼ , as shown in the illustration. During this process, genes are exchanged between male and female **2** Select . . . ▼ . In this way, both the sperm cell and the egg cell receive a new combination of genes, and the offspring will have new traits that are not identical to those of either parent.

1 Select . . . ▼

   A. crossing over

   B. mitotic division

   C. DNA replication

   D. genetic variation

1 Select . . . ▼

   A. sperm cells

   B. alternative genes

   C. complex molecules

   D. matching chromosomes

Genetic Expression and the Environment

The chemical environment of a cell can have an effect on the cellular processes that regulate gene expression. These environmentally induced changes can affect physical characteristics.

Directions: Use the passage below to answer questions 7–9.

Genetic Engineering

Detailed knowledge of DNA, genes, and chromosomes is relatively new because of the complex technology scientists needed to study such small structures. However, that does not mean that the study of genetics is new. For thousands of years, people have been using their observations to breed plants and animals with specific traits. This technique is called selective breeding. Nevertheless, the process takes time, and changes occur slowly over several generations. A faster and more complex method of controlling the genetic makeup of an organism is genetic engineering. This is the deliberate alteration of the structure of genetic material in a living organism.

One method of genetic engineering involves cutting a portion of the DNA from one organism and inserting it into another organism. DNA formed by combining pieces from different sources is described as recombinant (ree KAHM buhnunt) DNA. Scientists generally transfer DNA from a more complex organism to a simpler one. For example, they might transfer DNA from a human to a bacterial cell.

The organism into which the recombinant DNA is inserted is known as the host organism. The host organism uses the foreign DNA as if it were its own. When the bacteria reproduce, a copy of the DNA in a cell is made. The cell then divides into two cells that are identical to the original cell. When a bacterial cell containing human DNA reproduces, the cells produced also contain human DNA.

Why would scientists want to insert human DNA into bacteria? One reason is to produce substances that humans need. Insulin is a protein humans need to control the level of sugar in the blood. People with a condition known as diabetes must take injections of insulin every day. Genetically engineering bacterial cells that produce human insulin creates a plentiful supply of needed insulin.

7. By which process would the bacterial cell reproduce?

   A. meiosis

   B. mutation

   C. replication

   D. epigenetics

8. As used in the passage above, the word **trait** means _____ .

9. The cell containing the foreign DNA reproduces once, twice, and a third time. How many of the eight resulting cells will contain the foreign DNA?

   A. all of them

   B. six of them

   C. two of them

   D. half of them

This lesson will help you practice working with concepts related to natural selection and adaptation. Use it with core lesson 4.5 Selection and Adaptation to reinforce and apply your knowledge.

Key Concept

Through natural selection, adaptations evolve. Natural selection explains how species change over time and how new species arise.

Core Skills & Practices

- Reconcile Multiple Findings, Conclusions, or Theories
- Draw Conclusions

Natural Selection

Natural selection is a process by which organisms that are best adapted to their environment tend to survive and pass on genetic characteristics to their offspring.

Directions: Answer the following questions.

1. What observation did Darwin most likely make about tortoises living on the Galápagos Islands that caused him to question how species evolve?

   A. They all lived only on land.

   B. They were not highly vulnerable to predators.

   C. Their necks were different lengths and their shells were different shapes.

   D. The offspring had a high mortality rate.

2. What relationship did Charles Darwin recognize regarding the 13 different species of finches he observed?

   A. Beak shape was related to food type.

   B. Bone density was related to migration patterns.

   C. Leg length was related to ability to escape predators.

   D. Feather color was related to flora found in the environment.

3. A genetic mutation in a moth results in the moth emitting a new scent. Write A, B, C, and D in the appropriate box below to identify the correct sequence in the process of natural selection.

1.	
2.	
3.	
4.	

   A. Two distinct species of moths with specific scents develop.

   B. Many male moths are very attracted to the female moth emitting the new scent.

   C. Offspring of the moth with the new scent produce a growing population of moths with the scent, while the population of moths with the original scent gets smaller.

   D. The moth populations interbreed in captivity but in the wild breed only with their kind.

Adaptations

An adaptation is any trait that helps an organism survive and reproduce in its environment.

Directions: Answer the following questions.

4. Which is an example of mimicry?

 A. a stick insect that looks like the twigs found on the tree where it lives

 B. a hare whose fur changes from brown to white in the winter

 C. a nonpoisonous pine snake vibrating its tail like a poisonous rattle snake

 D. a rose plant that produces brightly colored flowers to which bees are attracted

5. On the Galápagos Islands, Darwin observed that finches that ate large seeds had a thick beak, while those that ate small seeds had a much thinner beak. What would happen to the finch population on an island where all the birds had thick beaks if the seeds they eat suddenly became much smaller?

 A. The birds would feed on other types of seeds because their beaks are thicker.

 B. The birds would reproduce with smaller beaked bird species to pass on the small beak trait.

 C. The birds would need to evolve to have smaller beaks to feed on the smaller seeds.

 D. The birds would find it difficult to survive because their beaks are not suited for smaller seeds.

Directions: Read the passage below. Then choose the option that correctly completes each sentence.

6. Many adaptations help to protect organisms from predators. An important adaptation is 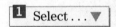, which helps an organism blend into the surrounding environment. Another important adaptation is 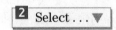, the ability of a harmless organism to look like a different, more dangerous organism.

1 Select . . . ▼

 A. mimicry

 B. camouflage

 C. bright coloration

 D. protective covering

2 Select . . . ▼

 A. mimicry

 B. camouflage

 C. bright coloration

 D. protective covering

✓ Test-Taking Tip

The more you practice reading different types of texts of different lengths, the better prepared you will be to read and understand passages presented in reading tests. A good way to practice is to read as much as you can about subjects that interest you. Not only will you become a better reader when taking a test, you will also increase your enjoyment of reading.

Speciation

Speciation is a process that results in a new species of organism arising from a parent organism.

Directions: Answer the following question.

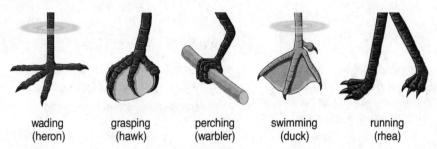

wading	grasping	perching	swimming	running
(heron)	(hawk)	(warbler)	(duck)	(rhea)

7. A scientist studying the birds shown in the image notes that both ducks and herons spend a great deal of time in the water. The scientist also observes that the foot structures of the two birds are very different. Which explanation can be used to reconcile these findings?

   A. The webbed feet of the duck are suited to swimming. A heron walks through water instead of swimming, so it needs a foot structure better suited for wading.

   B. Ducks need to swim to obtain their food from the water, but herons feed on small animals that live at the shoreline, so they do not need to have a foot structure that allows them to move easily in shallow water.

   C. A heron spends its time in the water only at the shoreline, so it does not need a foot structure that helps to move it through the water. The webbed feet of ducks allow the birds to live for long periods of time in the water.

   D. The structure of the heron's feet is well suited for wading, but the webbing of the duck's feet increase the surface area of the foot making it very well suited for walking on rocky shorelines with ease.

Directions: Use the passage below to answer questions 8–9.

> Marsupials in Australia evolved from the same ancestor. Kangaroos and koalas are both marsupials, but they are very different animals. Kangaroos are large animals that move on two powerful hind legs that help them travel long distances to find food. As they move, kangaroos also make use of large, powerful tails, which they use for balance and for defense. Koalas are far smaller marsupials that climb trees in order to find eucalyptus leaves to eat.

8. How are kangaroos and koalas examples of adaptive radiation? Explain your response.

   _____

   _____

   _____

   _____

9. Kangaroos and koalas are separate species. What trait needs to occur in order for two species that evolved from a common ancestor to be considered separate species?

   A. The two species have to have different feeding habits.

   B. The two species must look different from each other.

   C. The two species are not able to reproduce viable offspring with each other.

   D. The two species cannot survive in the same habitat anymore.

This lesson will help you practice working with concepts related to motion, momentum, and momentum conservation. Use it with core lesson 5.1 Motion to reinforce and apply your knowledge.

Key Concept

Objects are in motion all around us. Motion can be described by speed, velocity, and acceleration. A moving object has momentum, which can be transferred between objects during a collision.

Core Skills & Practices

• Express Scientific Information or Findings Numerically or Symbolically
• Interpret Graphs and Functions

Describing Motion

Motion can be described in terms of position, speed, velocity, and acceleration.

Directions: Use the graph below to answer questions 1–3.

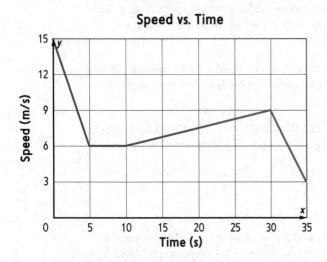

Speed vs. Time

1. The graph shows the change in speed of a car over time as the car moves along a straight street. At which time is the car's speed 7.8 m/s?

   A. 2 s

   B. 10 s

   C. 22 s

   D. 34 s

2. During which time intervals does the car undergo deceleration?

   A. 0–5 s and 5–10 s

   B. 0–5 s and 30–35 s

   C. 5–10 s and 10–30 s

   D. 10–30 s and 30–35 s

3. What is the magnitude of the car's acceleration between 10 s and 30 s?

   $$\text{acceleration} = \frac{(\text{final velocity} - \text{initial velocity})}{(\text{final time} - \text{initial time})}$$

   A. 0.15 m/s²

   B. 0.60 m/s²

   C. 0.90 m/s²

   D. 1.50 m/s²

Directions: Answer the questions below.

4. A plane flying east travels 75 km in 9.0 min. What is the plane's velocity?

$$\text{velocity} = \frac{(\text{final position} - \text{initial position})}{(\text{final time} - \text{initial time})}$$

A. 2.3 m/s, east

B. 0.3 m/s, east

C. 139 km/h, east

D. 500 km/h, east

5. A rolling grocery cart has no acceleration. Knowing just this, what information about velocity and speed can you infer about the cart's motion? What would be different if the cart were at rest?

_____

_____

_____

_____

Momentum

Momentum is defined as the product of an object's mass and velocity.

Directions: Use the graph below to answer questions 6–7.

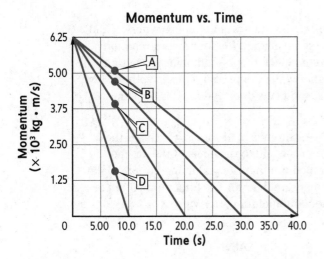

6. Suppose you are designing a device that safely reduces the momentum associated with an impact, such as what a safety helmet or airbag does for cyclists and motorists. From the graph shown, what can you infer about any design that uses a given amount of force to decrease momentum?

A. The materials of which the device is made need to be made as rigid as possible.

B. The materials of which the device is made need to be made as flexible as possible.

C. The time over which momentum decreases needs be made as large as possible.

D. The time over which momentum decreases needs be made as small as possible.

7. Which point on the graph indicates a momentum with magnitude of about 4,700 kg • m/s after 7.50 s have elapsed?

   A. Point A   C. Point C

   B. Point B   D. Point D

✓ Test-Taking Tip

When completing a "hot spot" activity in a computer-based exam, only certain points or regions on the diagram will be active. You must click on the point or region to answer the question. Identifying the possible hot spots will help narrow the possibilities for the answer.

Directions: Answer the questions below.

8. What is the momentum of an ice skater with a mass of 52.0 kg, and who is sliding with a velocity of 4.5 m/s to the south?

momentum = mass × velocity

A. 116 kg • m/s, south

B. 11.6 kg • m/s, south

C. 234 kg • m/s, south

D. 2,340 kg • m/s, south

9. A student stands on a skateboard with a bucket full of water. Everything is initially at rest. The student then tosses the water out of the bucket. If the student/bucket/skateboard/water system has a total mass of 80.0 kg, and the water has a mass of 10.0 kg and an initial velocity of 2.50 m/s, south, what is the final velocity of the student, skateboard, and bucket?

momentum = mass × velocity

A. 0.313 m/s, north   C. 0.357 m/s, north

B. 0.313 m/s, south   D. 0.357 m/s, south

Law of Conservation of Momentum

Momentum is conserved in all collisions, provided no force is applied to the system of colliding objects.

Directions: Use the reading passage and diagram below to answer questions 10–11.

What happens when an object exerts a force on a second object? Imagine what happens when a child kicks a door shut. The foot exerts a force on the door. At the same instant, the foot feels a reaction force from the door. When an object exerts a force on a second object, the second object exerts an equal force in the opposite direction on the first object. Another way of expressing this is with the law of conservation of momentum. The total momentum of the system (the door and foot) is the same before and after a collision.

A balloon rocket demonstrates momentum conservation. The difference in air pressure causes the air inside the balloon to move to the left rapidly. Its momentum is equal to the mass of the air and the velocity with which it escapes. The balloon moves with a momentum that is equal in magnitude to that of the air and is in the opposite direction (to the right in the diagram below). The total momentum of the air-balloon system before the air is released equals the total momentum afterward.

Before

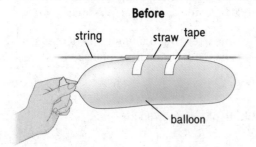

string   straw tape

balloon

After

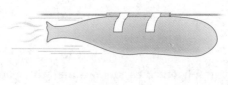

10. Suppose the mass of the balloon equals 0.010 kg, and the balloon moves to the right with a uniform speed of 0.10 m/s. The total momentum (momentum = mass × velocity) of the balloon-air system is 0 kg • m/s. How does the definition of momentum conservation tell you how this problem can be solved?

_____

_____

_____

11. Suppose the balloon-air system has an initial momentum toward the right. Which statement correctly describes how the system behaves after the air has been released from the balloon?

A. The balloon will move to the left.

B. The balloon will move faster to the right.

C. The balloon will move slower to the right.

D. The balloon's motion will not be affected.

This lesson will help you practice working with concepts related to forces and Newton's Laws of Motion and to understand how they affect the motion of everyday objects. Use it with core lesson 5.2 Forces and Newton's Laws of Motion to reinforce and apply your knowledge.

Key Concept

Newton's Laws describe the motion of objects. Newton's law of universal gravitation relates the mass and distance between two objects to the force of gravity between two objects. These laws can be used to predict the motion of everyday objects.

Core Skills & Practices

• Apply Formulas from Scientific Theories
• Solve Linear Equations

Newton's Laws of Motion

Newton's Laws of Motion can be used to predict the motion of objects in response to forces.

Directions: Use the diagram below to answer questions 1–2.

1. The man exerts a force of 40 N on the table (F_A), while the woman exerts a force of 60 N (F_B). The net force (F_{net}) acting on the table is _____ .

2. Assume that the man and the woman each exert a force of 60 N on the table in the same direction. In response to this force, the table moves a total distance of 10 meters. What is the acceleration of the table?

A. 5 m/s   C. 12 m/s²

B. 5 m/s²   D. 50 N/s

 Test-Taking Tip

Some multiple choice questions will require you to make calculations. When answering such questions, remember to check the units in your final answer.

Directions: Answer the questions below.

3. Four people are pushing grocery carts in a supermarket. Which cart has the greatest inertia?

A. an 8-kg cart being pushed by a child

B. a full grocery cart with a mass of 10 kg

C. an empty grocery cart with a mass of 5 kg

D. a half-full grocery cart with a mass of 20 kg

4. As a person rows a boat, the force exerted on the oars is transferred as an action force to the water. Why does the boat begin to move through the water rather than remain in one place? Use Newton's third law of motion to justify your response.

_____

_____

_____

_____

_____

5. What is the average acceleration of a 30-kg box that is pushed with 15 N and 30 N of force?

A. 0.5 m/s²

B. 1.0 m/s²

C. 1.5 m/s²

D. 0.75 m/s²

6. How are the forces of gravity and magnetism different from that of friction?

_____

_____

_____

_____

Directions: Use the diagram below to answer questions 7–8.

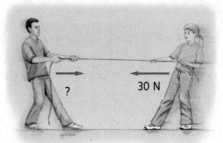

?   30 N

7. The people shown are having a tug-of-war. The person on the left is exerting a pulling force of 30 N on the rope toward the left. If the rope is moving toward the person on the left, what can you conclude about the force being exerted on the rope by the person on the right? Explain your answer.

_____

_____

_____

_____

8. What conclusion can be drawn if the rope in the tug-of-war game shown does not move toward either the right or the left?

A. The forces acting on the rope are unbalanced.

B. A net force of 30 N to the right is acting on the rope.

C. A force less than of 30 N is pulling the rope toward the right.

D. The forces acting on the rope are balanced and the net force is 0.

The Law of Universal Gravitation

The universal law of gravitation explains how gravity exerts a force between any two objects that have mass.

Directions: Use the diagram below to answer questions 9–10.

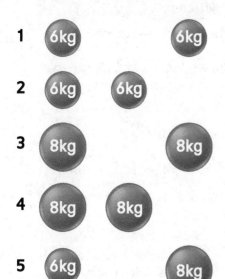

9. The diagram shows five pairs of balls. The gravitational force is weakest between the balls shown in pair number _____ and strongest between the balls shown in pair number _____ .

10. Currently the balls in pairs 1, 3, and 5 are the same distance apart. If the distance between the balls in each of these three pairs is doubled, then the force of gravity exerted on the balls in each pair will **1** Select . . . ▼ . If the mass of only one ball in pair 1, 3, or 5 were doubled, the force of gravity acting upon the balls in each pair would **2** Select . . . ▼ .

1 Select . . . ▼

A. remain the same

B. increase by one-half

C. decrease by one-half

D. decrease by one-fourth

2 Select . . . ▼

A. double

B. remain the same

C. increase by one-half

D. decrease by one-half

Directions: Use the formula $W = mg$ to answer the questions below.

11. If a person has a mass of 50 kg, what is this person's weight?

A. 5.1 N

B. 50 kg

C. 490 N

D. 490 kg

12. A person on Earth has a weight of 539 N. On Jupiter, this person's weight is 1,273.8 N. Which correctly identifies both the mass of the individual and the acceleration due to gravity on Jupiter?

A. 55 N; 9.8 m/s^2

B. 55 kg; 9.8 m/s^2

C. 55 N; 23.16 m/s^2

D. 55 kg; 23.16 m/s^2

Lesson 5.3 Work and Simple Machines

This lesson will help you practice working with concepts related to work and simple machines. Use it with core lesson 5.3 Work and Simple Machines to reinforce and apply your knowledge.

Key Concept

When forces move an object over a distance, work has been done. Simple machines are used to make work easier by reducing either the force or the distance. Compound machines are made of more than one simple machine.

Core Skills & Practices

• Identify and Refine Hypotheses for Scientific Investigations
• Follow a Multistep Procedure and Analyze the Results

Work and Power

Work is done when a force moves an object some distance in the same direction as the force is exerted.

Directions: Answer the questions below.

1. Which of the following measurements might represent an amount of work done on an object?

   A. 14.2 J

   B. 68.0 N

   C. 71.3 W

   D. 95.6 m/s^2

2. A horizontal force causes an object with a mass of 10 kg to accelerate at 4 m/s^2 and move a distance of 30 m horizontally. How much work is done by the force?

   $$F = ma \quad W = Fd$$

   A. 40 J

   B. 70 J

   C. 300 J

   D. 1,200 J

3. Several students took turns exerting a horizontal force on a desk initially resting on the floor. The force (F) and the horizontal distance (d) the desk moved as a result of that force are listed for each student. Write the names of the students in the boxes to order them from the least to the greatest amount of work done on the desk.

$$W = Fd$$

Sarina	Carlos	Sameel	Trey
F= 10 N; d= 9 m	F= 8 N; d= 12 m	F= 15 N; d= 5 m	F= 20 N; d= 3 m

LEAST			GREATEST
1.	2.	3.	4.

✔ Test-Taking Tip

When a test requires you to put items in an order sequence, it is sometimes helpful to start with the first and last answers. Find the last item or the final result. Then find the first item or the first result. Continue until you have all the items placed in order. Then look at the items from the first item to the last to make sure that each item would cause the next item to happen.

Machines

Machines make work easier to do by either reducing the amount of force that must be exerted or decreasing the distance over which the force is exerted.

Directions: Answer the questions below.

4. Which pair of simple machines is most closely related?

   A. levers and wedges

   B. wedges and screws

   C. screws and pulleys

   D. inclined planes and wheels and axles

5. A group of students conducts an investigation using a ramp and a box. They begin with the hypothesis that the amount of work they need to do to lift the box to a shelf 0.5 m above the ground will decrease as the length of the ramp increases. They lift the box with a spring scale and record the distance they pull it and the force they use. Their data are summarized in the table.

Distance	Force
0.5 m	20.0 N
0.8 m	12.5 N
1.0 m	10.0 N
1.5 m	6.67 N

How should they revise their hypothesis based on their results? Explain your reasoning.

_____

_____

_____

_____

Directions: Use the diagram below to answer questions 6–7.

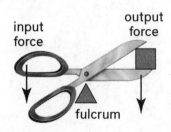 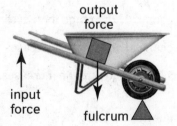 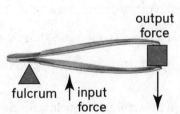

6. The illustration shows three types of levers. Explain two ways the levers are alike.

   _____

   _____

   _____

7. Circle the type of lever that always magnifies the distance over which a force is exerted.

Analyze Machine Use

The mechanical advantage of a machine is the ratio of the output force to the input force.

Directions: Answer the questions below.

8. A carpenter applies a force of 60 N to pry a nail out of a wooden beam. The hammer applies a force of 720 N to the nail. What is the mechanical advantage of the hammer?

$$MA = \text{output force} / \text{input force}$$

A. 12   C. 640

B. 56   D. 780

9. What is true about the mechanical advantage of a machine that increases the distance over which a force must be exerted to complete a task?

A. MA = 0   C. MA < 1

B. MA = 1   D. MA > 1

10. A pair of students designs an investigation to test a hypothesis. They attach a weight to the end of a wooden beam and allow it to pivot around a rock. The students attach a spring scale to the free end and pull down on the scale to lift the weight. The students hypothesize that the closer the rock is to the spring scale, the lower the force they measure will be. The average force over several trials for each setup is listed in the table.

Setup	Force
A	53 N
B	71N
C	98N

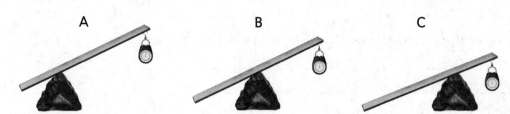

A   B   C

The students' hypothesis was not supported by the data. If the distance between the weight and the fulcrum is x and the distance between the fulcrum and the spring scale is y, the students should revise their hypothesis to which of the following based on their results?

A. If the ratio of x to y is 1, then the mechanical advantage will be greatest.

B. If the ratio of y to x increases, then the mechanical advantage increases.

C. If the ratio of x to y increases, then the mechanical advantage increases.

D. If the ratio of y to x decreases, then the mechanical advantage increases.

Directions: Use the information below to answer questions 11–12.

A boat mechanic uses a pulley system to lift an engine into place. The mechanic exerts a force of 900 N to lift the 1800 N engine. $MA = \text{output force} / \text{input force}$

11. What is the mechanical advantage of the pulley system?

A. 2   C. 9

B. 6   D. 18

12. If the mechanic alters the design of the pulley system, the mechanical advantage becomes 6. The force that will be required to lift the engine will be _____.

This lesson will help you practice working with concepts related to different types of energy and the transformation of energy from one type to another. Use it with core lesson 6.1 Types of Energy and Energy Transformations to reinforce and apply your knowledge.

Key Concept

There are many types of energy that cause changes in the world around us. Energy of one type can be transformed into energy of another type, but the total amount of energy cannot be changed.

Core Skills and Practices

- Interpret Meaning of Mathematical Symbols
- Identify the Strengths and Weaknesses of a Scientific Investigation Design

What Is Energy?

Energy is the ability to do work or make things happen. Every action is connected to energy in one form or another. Objects can have energy due to either their movement or their position.

Directions: Answer the questions below.

1. A skateboard at the top of a ramp represents which of the following types of potential energy?

   A. elastic

   B. magnetic

   C. electrical

   D. gravitational

3. A student sets a computer with a mass of 6.50 kg on a shelf 3.20 m above the floor. How much gravitational potential energy does the computer have with respect to the floor?

   A. 204 J

   B. 4.82 J

   C. 20.8 J

   D. 63.7 J

2. In an experiment designed to test the energy efficiencies of several skateboards, the kinetic energies have been measured, along with the speeds and masses of the boards. Use the formula $KE = \frac{1}{2} mv^2$, and the speeds and mass values provided to complete the table.

   | 4.00 m/s | 2.50 m/s | 1.50 kg | 0.75 kg | 1.50 m/s |

KE (J)	Mass (kg)	Speed (m/s)
6.00		
4.69		
12.00		
2.34		
0.844		

  Test-Taking Tip

When answering a drag-and-drop question, it is important to read the question carefully before selecting items. When you are sure you understand the question, carefully read the items to select. First, select the items you feel confident you know; then go back and work on the items about which you are less sure.

Types of Energy

Many types of kinetic and potential energy, can take a different form under the appropriate conditions. Mechanic, thermal, chemical, nuclear and radiant are all types of energy.

Directions: Use the diagram below to answer questions 4–5.

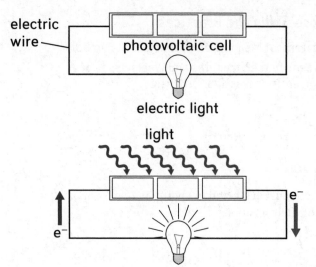

4. A photovoltaic cell uses energy from

_____ .

5. What is the purpose of a photovoltaic cell?

A. to change electrical energy into radiant energy

B. to change radiant energy into electrical energy

C. to change radiant energy into chemical energy

D. to change chemical energy into electrical energy

Electrical Energy and Magnetic Energy

Some forms of energy can affect objects from a distance due to a field that exists around the energy source. Electrical energy and magnetic energy are both produced by fields. These forms of energy are related to one another.

Directions: Use the passage and diagram below to answer questions 6–7.

In 1813, the Danish physicist and chemist Hans Christian Ørsted predicted that a connection soon would be found between electricity and magnetism. In 1820, he found that connection when he discovered that a current-carrying wire was surrounded by a magnetic field. The strength of the field depended on the distance from the wire and on the amount of electric current. Ørsted's discovery helped scientists understand electric current, which they believed was a type of electric fluid. However, electrons, the particles that produce electric current, would not be discovered until seventy-five years later.

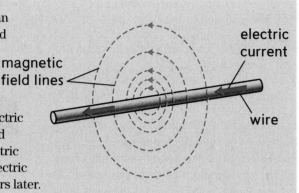

6. According to the passage, what can you infer about what scientists today believe gives rise to magnetism?

A. the movement of electrons

B. the strength of a magnetic field

C. the direction of electrostatic force

D. the number of copper atoms in a wire

7. Which of the following experiments could Ørsted have used to convince other scientists of his discovery?

A. A straight wire carrying current does not deflect a compass needle, but a coiled wire does.

B. A wire carrying current does not change its mass as the current is increased.

C. An iron nail, surrounded by a coil of wire carrying a current, does not attract iron.

D. A wire carrying current causes the needle of a nearby compass to deflect.

Conservation of Energy

Energy is neither created nor destroyed, but changes form from one type of energy to another. This is referred to as the law of conservation of energy.

Directions: Read the information below and examine the diagram and graph. Then answer questions 8–10.

A block slides without friction down a slick ramp, as shown in the figure below. The graph shows the values of both the gravitational potential energy (which depends only on the height of the block above the ground) and the kinetic energy as it slides.

8. Which statement about the block is true?

   A. Only half of the block's original potential energy is changed to kinetic energy.

   B. On the graph at the point where $d = 0$, the block's energy is all potential energy.

   C. On the graph at the point where $d = 0$, the block's energy is all kinetic energy.

   D. On the graph at the point where $d = 10$, half of the block's energy is kinetic energy.

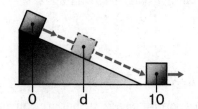

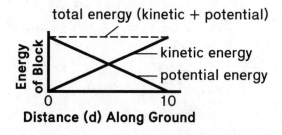

9. What remains constant as the block moves down the ramp?

   A. the difference between the block's potential energy and kinetic energy

   B. the total kinetic energy of the block

   C. the total potential energy of the block

   D. the sum of the block's potential energy and kinetic energy

10. Suppose the dotted line for total energy in the graph was not horizontal, but sloped downward toward the right. What would this indicate?

   _____

   _____

   _____

   _____

This lesson will help you practice working with concepts related to different types of energy resources used by humans. Use it with core lesson 6.2 Sources of Energy to reinforce and apply your knowledge.

Key Concept	Core Skills & Practices
There are many sources of energy. Which type of energy source people choose to use depends on each source's advantages and disadvantages.	• Distinguish Between Cause and Effect • Understand and Explain Textual Scientific Presentations

Sources of Energy

Energy resources are natural materials that are converted into energy forms that people can use.

Directions: Use the diagram to answer the question.

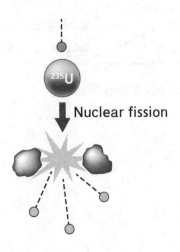

Nuclear fission

1. Uranium-235 is an isotope used in nuclear power plants. What happens when atoms of U-235 undergo nuclear fission?

   A. It will not change.

   B. It will split apart producing two more stable atoms and subatomic particles

   C. It will cause the nucleus to double in size.

   D. It will split apart creating two atoms that are identical.

Direction: Answer the following question.

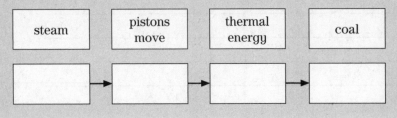

2. A steam engine can transform the energy stored in fuel into kinetic energy. Complete the table by writing the terms in order to show each step in the process when a steam engine provides energy.

steam	pistons move	thermal energy	coal

 Test-Taking Tip

When a test requires you to put steps or items in a cause-and-effect sequence, it is sometimes helpful to work backwards. Find the last item or the final result. Then work backwards from there. Continue until you have all the items placed in order.

Many of Earth's natural energy sources, such as coal, are finite. Our goal is to use more renewable non-polluting energy sources. It will take time to reach that goal. However as we move toward that goal we should consider making nonrenewable nuclear energy one of our main energy choices.

3. Which information about nuclear energy supports this statement?

   A. Use of nuclear energy does not pollute the air.

   B. Generating nuclear energy is the only use for uranium.

   C. No waste is produced when nuclear energy is generated.

   D. Nuclear energy is safe and poses no threat to the environment

4. The word **finite** as used in the statement means

   _____ .

5. Based on the statement, you can infer that the use of natural energy sources causes

   _____ .

Renewable Energy Resources

Energy resources that are inexhaustible, or that can be replaced as they are used, are renewable energy resources.

Direction: Answer the following questions.

6. Which renewable energy resource can cause air pollution?

   A. biomass

   B. wind energy

   C. solar energy

   D. geothermal energy

7. Some people worry that too much land might be used for the growth of crops than can be converted to ethanol, such as corn and switch grass. They think that using the land to provide energy resources could cause other problems. What might be their concern?

   A. This practice could cause food shortage.

   B. This practice could put farmers out of work.

   C. There could not be enough seeds for the plants.

   D. There could not be enough workers for these farms.

8. Which renewable energy resource can be used nearly anywhere?

   A. wind

   B. water.

   C. biomass

   D. geothermal

9. A town council wants to pass building rules that would require each new house built to use a renewable energy source for its heating and cooling systems. If you were the mayor in that town would you support the bill? Justify your answer.

   _____

   _____

   _____

   _____

   _____

Choosing Sources of Energy

When choosing an energy source, many factors need to be studied, including the availability of the energy source, the cost of the energy source, and its impact on the environment.

Direction: Use the graph below to answer questions 10–11.

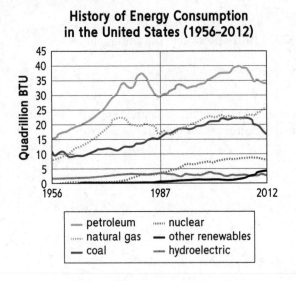

History of Energy Consumption in the United States (1956–2012)

10. Look at the lines for the consumption of petroleum and natural gas. If the usage patterns continue, about when will the United States use more natural gas than petroleum?

   A. 2012

   B. 2020

   C. 2030

   D. 2040

11. When combined, which uses of energy sources equal the current use of petroleum?

   A. coal and nuclear

   B. coal and natural gas

   C. nuclear and natural gas

   D. other renewables and natural gas

Directions: Use the passage below to answer questions 12–13.

> The technological advances needed to develop safe, affordable energy sources cost a great deal of money, much of which will be paid by taxpayers. For these reasons, the safety of energy production in the United States and elsewhere in the world depends on what we, as citizens, are willing to tolerate. In modern society, pollution control and technological advancement are political questions as well as scientific ones.

12. According to the passage above, why is pollution control a "political question as well as a scientific one?"

   A. because it involves taxpayer money

   B. because it involves safety of energy production

   C. because it involves affordable energy sources

   D. because it involves technological advances

13. Fracking is a technological advancement that can be used to increase the supply of natural gas but may cause environmental damage. Why might a technological advancement like this have political considerations?

   _____

   _____

   _____

   _____

   _____

This lesson will help you practice working with concepts related to heat and the transfer of energy as heat. Use it with core lesson 6.3 Heat to reinforce and apply your knowledge.

Key Concept

When thermal energy is added to a substance, there is an increased movement of the particles that make up the substance. More movement of the particles means an increased kinetic energy. This increased kinetic energy can be transferred to other parts of the substance and to other substances.

Core Skills & Practices

- Express Scientific Information or Findings Verbally
- Evaluate Evidence

Principles of Heat

Heat is the transfer of thermal energy, which is a measure of the kinetic and potential energy of the particles that make up a substance.

Directions: Use the passage below to answer questions 1–2.

Heat is the transfer of the kinetic energy caused by the movement of atoms and molecules. When these particles move rapidly, an object feels hot. When they move slowly, the object feels cold. A more precise way of measuring the average kinetic energy of these particles is temperature. When heat transfers energy to an object, the temperature of the object increases. When the object gives off energy by heat, its temperature decreases.

When two objects of different temperature are brought into contact with each other, heat flows from the object at higher temperature to the object at lower temperature. Heat continues to flow until both objects reach the same temperature. When this occurs, the average kinetic energy of the particles of both objects is also the same.

1. Which statement best describes the nature of heat?

   A. the transfer of the kinetic energy of an object's atoms or molecules

   B. the flow of energy between two objects in contact and at the same temperature

   C. the total energy contained within an object

   D. the measure of the temperature of an object

2. When a piece of hot iron (98° C) is thrown into a barrel of cold water (22° C), what will happen?

   A. Heat will flow from the water to the iron until both are the same temperature.

   B. Heat will flow from the iron to the water until both are the same temperature.

   C. The temperature of the iron will decrease until it reaches 22° C.

   D. The temperature of the water will increase until it reaches 98° C.

Direction: Answer the question below.

3. The data in the upper row of the table indicate the average kinetic energy of a substance. Sort the temperatures given by writing each temperature value in the appropriate space below the corresponding energy value.

90K	155K	205K	575K	1140K

Energy	4.3×10^{-21} J	2.4×10^{-20} J	1.9×10^{-21} J	3.2×10^{-21} J	1.2×10^{-20} J
Temperature					

✓ Test-Taking Tip

When completing a sorting activity such as the one above, note whether the two sets of values being compared increase together or decrease together, or whether one decreases as the other increases. Once this has been determined, find the greatest or smallest values that correspond to the given quantities, and use the ratio between any two given values to find how the remaining numbers relate to each other.

Kinetic Heat Transfer

Heat can be transferred by one of three processes: conduction, convection, and radiation. Conduction involves the transfer of heat through a material by means of atomic or molecular motion. Convection involves the displacement of hot and cold fluids because of their different densities. Radiation involves energy transfer by electromagnetic radiation, which can travel through a vacuum.

Direction: Use the image below to answer question 4.

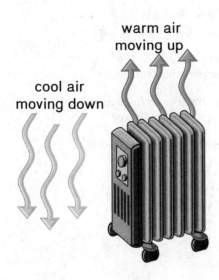

warm air moving up

cool air moving down

4. Which statement describes the role of conduction in the radiator shown in the illustration?

A. Electromagnetic waves transfer energy from the radiator surface to the air at its sides.

B. Electromagnetic waves transfer energy from the fluid inside the radiator to its surface.

C. Heat transfers energy from the fluid inside the radiator to its surface.

D. Heat transfers energy by convection to the air at the sides of the radiator.

Directions: Answer the questions below.

5. What happens to a heated fluid as convection occurs?

    A. Increased motion pushes the particles of heated fluid upward past particles of the unheated fluid.

    B. Increased particle motion causes the fluid to sink and displace the surrounding unheated fluid upward.

    C. Increased particle motion causes the fluid to expand and become less dense than unheated fluid.

    D. The heated fluid radiates energy away and becomes less dense than the surrounding unheated fluid.

6. Electrons move easily through the crystal structure of substance A. They do not move freely at all in substance B. Which statement predicts accurately the heat transfer properties of each substance?

    A. Substance A will conduct heat more easily than substance B.

    B. Substance B will conduct heat more easily than substance A.

    C. Substance A will more easily transfer heat by convection than substance B.

    D. Substance B will more easily transfer heat by convection than substance A.

Energy Conversions Involving Heat

Mechanical energy can be converted to heat, and heat can be converted to mechanical energy. Friction between surfaces is one of the more common ways in which mechanical energy in the form of kinetic energy is converted to heat.

Directions: Answer the following questions.

7. Suppose you are preparing for a long drive and need to fill your tires with air. Why is it important not to overinflate tires when they are cool?

    A. The pressure from the air inside the tire causes the rubber of the tire to overheat, which can cause a possible blowout.

    B. The heat radiated from the road through the rubber tire causes the air in the tire to expand, and possibly cause the tire to blow out.

    C. Heat from the friction between the tires and the road will cause the air in the tire to expand, and possibly cause the tire to blow out.

    D. Heat from the friction between the tires and the road causes air surrounding the tire to heat and form convection currents that can result in a blowout.

8. Water is often sprayed on high-speed drill bits to lower their temperature during the drilling process. Which of the following gives the best explanation, in terms of energy conversion, for why this is necessary?

    A. The kinetic energy of the bit is converted into heat by the friction between the bit and drilled substance.

    B. Thermal energy is conducted by heat from the drilled substance to the bit.

    C. Thermal energy is conducted by heat away from the bit to the air.

    D. Thermal energy is converted to mechanical energy by friction, which causes the drill to operate less effectively.

This lesson will help you practice working with concepts related to waves and the transfer of energy by waves. Use it with core lesson 6.4 Waves to reinforce and apply your knowledge.

Key Concept	Core Skills & Practices
Waves carry energy that spreads out as the wave travels. There are different types of waves that all exhibit properties of wavelength, frequency, and amplitude.	• Determine Details • Use Data or Evidence to Form a Conclusion

The Nature of Waves

A wave is a repeating disturbance that transfers energy as it travels through matter or space. Sound waves, ocean waves, light waves, and radio waves are all types of waves.

Directions: Answer the questions below.

1. Which feature is characteristic of a wave?

   A. the presence of light

   B. the presence of sound

   C. the presence of vibration

   D. the presence of a liquid medium

2. What evidence demonstrates that energy is transferred by a wave?

   A. Energy passing through a medium is always accompanied by light energy from the source.

   B. Energy causes a disturbance that is passed through a medium, and energy must be conserved.

   C. Energy pushes matter through the medium in the form of a disturbance, or wave.

   D. Energy, which is conserved, disturbs and is conveyed by matter moving in the medium.

3. Use your knowledge of the nature of waves to explain why, when an explosion occurs, you hear a "boom" and, at the same time, the windows rattle.

   _____

   _____

   _____

   _____

   _____

4. You observe a disturbance on the surface of a lake. A buoy floats on the lake's surface. Describe what evidence you would have to observe in order to conclude that the disturbance is a wave.

   _____

   _____

   _____

   _____

   _____

Wave Types and Their Properties

Waves can be either transverse or longitudinal and possess the properties of wave speed, frequency, wavelength, and amplitude.

Directions: Use the diagram below to answer questions 5–6.

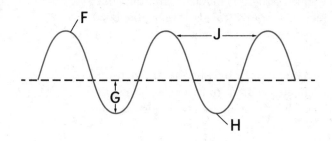

5. If the wave in the figure is moving up and down with a frequency of 25 Hz, and the wavelength is 0.030 m, what is the correct value for the speed of the wave?

   A. 1.3 m/s

   B. 830 m/s

   C. 0.75 m/s

   D. 0.0012 m/s

6. Point F indicates the 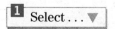 of the wave, whereas point H indicates the 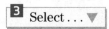 of the wave. These displacements in a **3** Select... ▼ wave are a measure of the distance from the rest position, which is called the **4** Select... ▼ of the wave. This property of a wave, indicated by the point, is related to the amount of energy that the wave transfers.

1 Select... ▼

A. crest

B. trough

C. amplitude

D. wavelength

3 Select... ▼

A. transverse

B. rarefaction

C. compressed

D. longitudinal

2 Select... ▼

A. crest

B. trough

C. amplitude

D. wavelength

4 Select... ▼

A. crest

B. trough

C. amplitude

D. wavelength

✔ **Test-Taking Tip**

When answering a drop-down question, try to read the passage and think of the answer on your own before looking at the answer choices. This will help you quickly eliminate answer choices that do not fit the context of the passage.

The Electromagnetic Spectrum

Electromagnetic waves make up the electromagnetic spectrum, which includes visible light.

Directions: Use the passage below to answer questions 7–8.

> Although both light and sound are forms of wave energy, the speed of light is much greater than the speed of sound. Light travels at about 300,000 kilometers per second. Sound travels at only about 350 meters per second. One way to distinguish the difference between the speed of light and the speed of sound is to make observations during a lightning storm.
>
> Lightning is caused by separated electrical charges rushing together in the atmosphere. At the instant the charges come together, both a flash of light and a loud sound are created (thunder). Although the flash of lightning reaches your eyes almost at once, the sound of thunder may not reach your ears until several seconds later.
>
> You can use the relative speeds of light and sound to find out how far away the lightning is: when you see a flash of lightning, start counting slowly, spacing your counts one second apart. For each 3 seconds you count before you hear the thunder, you know that the lightning is about 1 kilometer away. If you see a flash and count 6 seconds before hearing thunder, the lightning flash occurred about 2 kilometers from you.

7. Assume you know that both light and sound are created at the instant that lightning occurs but that you do not know either the speed of light or the speed of sound. Which statement supports the understanding that light travels faster than sound?

   A. Light and sound are both independent of the properties of the medium.

   B. Light and sound are both forms of wave energy.

   C. As you move toward a lightning storm, the sound of thunder becomes fainter.

   D. You always see a lightning flash before you hear the thunder that is created with it.

8. Suppose the speed of light in air is 10,000 times slower than it is in a vacuum. What do you need to take into consideration if you see a flash of lightning and then hear thunder 30 seconds later?

   A. Light cannot be assumed to reach the observer instantaneously.

   B. Neither sound nor light can be detected after 30 seconds.

   C. The time of travel is very nearly the same for both types of waves.

   D. The distances traveled by the two different kinds of waves are different.

Direction: Answer the question below.

9. Which sequence of the wavelengths listed below correctly lists electromagnetic radiation in order from lowest to highest energy?

95 m	7.5×10^2 m	3.0×10^3 m	8.5×10^1 m
LOWEST ENERGY			HIGHEST ENERGY

This lesson will help you practice working with concepts related to the structure and properties of different kinds of matter and how elements are organized in the periodic table. Use it with core lesson 7.1 The Structure of Matter to reinforce and apply your knowledge.

Key Concept

All matter is made of atoms. Atoms of different elements have unique properties that determine the properties of the substance they make up.

Core Skills & Practices

- Understand and Explain Textual Scientific Presentations
- Apply Scientific Models

The Structure of Matter

Matter is anything that has mass and takes up space. All matter is made up of one or more elements, and each element is made up of atoms. Elements are represented by chemical symbols.

Directions: Answer the questions below.

1. Which question is most likely the subject of current scientific research on atomic structure?

    A. Where are neutrons and protons found in an atom?

    B. What is the role of subatomic particles in an atom?

    C. What charge do protons, neutrons, and electrons carry?

    D. Are atoms made of only protons, neutrons, and electrons?

2. Electrolysis uses electricity to decompose water (H_2O), forming the products hydrogen (H_2) and oxygen (O_2). How should the products resulting from the electrolysis of water be classified?

    A. atoms

    B. elements

    C. molecules

    D. compounds

Directions: Use the image below to answer question 3.

3. The image shows all of the particles that make up a helium atom. The overall electrical chart of the helium is _____. Explain your answer.

    _____

    _____

    _____

    _____

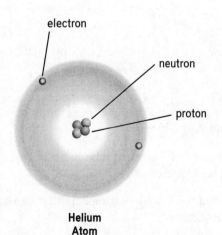

Helium
Atom

Periodic Table of the Elements

The periodic table of elements organizes elements according to similar chemical and physical properties. Each element has a square in the table that includes its name, chemical symbol, atomic number, atomic mass, and natural state.

Directions: Use the image below to answer questions 4–6.

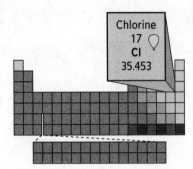

4. Which conclusion about chlorine is supported by its location in the periodic table?

A. Chlorine is a metal.

B. Chlorine is a nonmetal.

C. Chlorine is a metalloid.

D. Chlorine is a synthetic element.

5. Atoms of an element generally exist in a neutral state. Which part of chlorine's square in the periodic table provides information about the number of electrons that a neutral atom of chlorine has?

A. 17

B. Cl

C.

D. 35.453

6. Explain how information in the periodic table can be used to determine the number of neutrons in the nucleus of an atom of an element.

_____

_____

_____

_____

Directions: Use the passage to answer question 7.

- Elements are classified as metals, nonmetals, or metalloids, according to their properties.
- Metals—elements that are good conductors of electricity and are malleable (can be softened by striking with a hammer), shiny, and ductile (can be stretched)
- Nonmetals—elements that are not good conductors of electricity, and are not shiny, malleable, or ductile
- Metalloids—elements that have some of the properties of metals and some of the properties of nonmetals

7. You have a sample of an element that you think might be a metal. Which investigation could you use to determine if your sample is a metal?

A. Use the sample in place of a piece of wire in a working electrical circuit to see if the circuit continues to conduct electricity.

B. Compare the color of the unknown sample to that of a known metal to determine if the colors are shared by both substances.

C. Attempt to bend the sample using only your hands to determine if it shows the property of malleability.

D. Drop the sample into a container of water to determine if it sinks or floats. Repeat the process using oil instead of water and compare the results.

Compounds

When the atoms of two or more different elements combine chemically, they form a compound.

Directions: Answer the following questions.

8. Methane is a flammable, gaseous compound made up of only carbon (C) and hydrogen (H) atoms. The ratio of carbon to hydrogen in a methane molecule is 1 to 4. Which is the chemical formula for methane?

    A. C_4H

    B. CH_4

    C. $4CH$

    D. C_1H_4

9. Chalk is a compound formed when one atom of calcium combines with one atom of carbon and three atoms of oxygen. The chemical formula for chalk is _____.

Directions: Use the table below to answer question 10.

Data Table: Determining Iron Content by Mass

Sample	Original Mass	New Mass
1	0.50 g	0.62 g
2	0.50 g	0.51 g
3	0.50 g	0.901g
4	0.50 g	0.55 g

10. Iron oxide, or rust, is a compound that forms as a result of a chemical reaction between iron and oxygen. The reaction occurs more rapidly in the presence of water. Suppose you are provided with four 0.50 gram metal samples. The samples contain varying amounts of iron mixed with other less reactive metals. To determine which sample has the highest iron content, you decide to place each sample in separate Petri dishes that contain small, but equal amounts of tap water and place all of the samples in the same outdoor location. After 3 weeks, you measure the mass of each of sample and record it in a data table. Based upon the new masses, which of your original samples had the highest iron content?

_____

_____

_____

✔ Test-Taking Tip

Before answering a short answer question, rule out what the question is *not* asking. Then, organize your thoughts around what you do know about the topic. After you have written your answer, check back over the question to be sure you followed all directions accurately.

_____

This lesson will help you practice working with concepts related to the properties of matter. Use it with core lesson 7.2 Chemical and Physical Properties of Matter to reinforce and apply your knowledge.

Key Concept	Core Skills & Practices
Matter can be described by its physical properties and chemical properties. The properties of elements are similar within groups on the periodic table.	• Cite Textual Evidence • Evaluate Conclusions

Properties of Matter

Physical and chemical properties can be used to identify types of matter.

Directions: Answer the questions below.

1. A student is designing an investigation to identify a chemical property of matter. Which procedure would be most useful?

   A. bending a steel rod

   B. sawing a wooden board in half

   C. painting a sheet of metal a different color

   D. placing an antacid tablet in a beaker of water

2. A scientist is investigating the properties of an unknown sample. Which observation is most useful in identifying the sample?

   A. The sample reflects light.

   B. The mass of the sample is 56.8 g.

   C. The density of the sample is 10.49 g/cm^3.

   D. The sample tarnishes when exposed to air.

3. A student places a sample of salt crystals on a lab table and observes its physical properties. The student then removes half of the sample and again observes the physical properties of the sample. Some properties stayed the same and some changed. Using the properties listed, write the properties the student observed in the correct category of the chart.

Color	Volume	Mass
Temperature	Density	Shape

Stayed the Same	Changed

 Test-Taking Tip

When completing a drag and drop sorting item, read the directions carefully to make sure you understand the criteria you should use to sort the items. Read the headings of the categories provided. Then after you place the items in the categories, review your answers to make sure the items were placed in the correct categories.

Changes of State

Matter can change from one state to another when thermal energy is absorbed or released.

Directions: Use the diagram to answer questions 4–5.

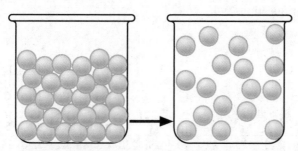

The diagram shows a sample of matter undergoing a change.

4. The sample begins in the _____ state and changes to the _____ state.

5. Explain how thermal energy is related to the change shown in the diagram.

   _____

   _____

   _____

   _____

Directions: Use the diagram to answer questions 6–8.

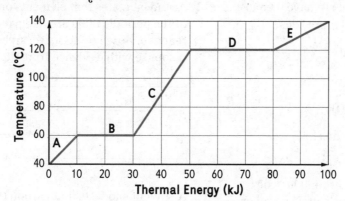

6. According to the graph, the melting point for the substance is _____ degrees and the boiling point is _____ degrees.

7. A student states that the temperature of a substance increases whenever thermal energy is absorbed. Evaluate this statement, and either support it or refute it using evidence from the graph.

   _____

   _____

   _____

   _____

8. Which processes are represented by section D?

   A. melting and freezing

   B. sublimation and boiling

   C. evaporation and sublimation

   D. vaporization and condensation

Predicting Properties

Knowing the location of an element on the periodic table makes it possible to predict its physical and chemical properties

Directions: Use the diagram to answer questions 9–12.

9. Which pair of elements is likely to have the most similar physical and chemical properties?

   A. iron (Fe) and cadmium (Cd)

   B. hydrogen (H) and helium (He)

   C. lithium (Li) and beryllium (Be)

   D. magnesium (Mg) and calcium (Ca)

10. Computer designers require certain kinds of materials to build the inner parts of a computer. To control the transmission of information, they need to use elements that can be made to conduct electricity under certain conditions but not others. Which of the following elements would be best suited for this purpose?

    A. iron (Fe)

    B. silicon (Si)

    C. xenon (Xe)

    D. rubidium (Rb)

11. A student states that elements on both sides of the periodic table are likely to be highly reactive. Agree or disagree, and support your response with evidence from the periodic table.

    _____

    _____

    _____

    _____

12. A student suggests that carbon (C) and lead (Pb) have similar properties because they are in the same group of the periodic table. Suggest a reason why their properties are very different.

    A. Carbon is a gas at room temperature whereas lead is a solid.

    B. Carbon has fewer outermost electrons than lead.

    C. Carbon is a nonmetal whereas lead is a metal.

    D. Carbon has fewer total electrons than lead.

This lesson will help you practice working with concepts related to chemical reactions. Use it with core lesson 7.3 Chemical Reactions to reinforce and apply your knowledge.

Key Concept

Changes in matter and energy occur during a chemical reaction, although matter is neither created nor destroyed. A balanced chemical equation shows the rearrangement of atoms and describes a chemical reaction.

Core Skills & Practices

- Identify and Reduce Sources of Error
- Determine Central Ideas

What Happens During a Chemical Reaction?

During a chemical reaction, one or more substances are changed into new substances.

Directions: Use the information to answer questions 1–2.

A student follows this procedure to conduct an investigation:

1. Use a funnel to half-fill a bottle with vinegar.
2. Determine the mass of the bottle with the vinegar.
3. Dry the funnel and use it to add 20 g of baking soda to the bottle.
4. Observe the chemical reaction that takes place.
5. After the reaction is complete, determine the mass of the bottle with its contents.

1. The student concludes that mass is not conserved because the mass after the reaction is less than the total mass before the reaction. What is one way the student can correct the error made during the investigation to produce the correct result?

   A. Add the baking soda to the bottle before the vinegar.

   B. Measure the mass of the vinegar and bottle separately.

   C. Decrease the mass of baking soda added to the vinegar.

   D. Stretch a balloon of known mass over the opening of the bottle.

2. Which of the following is an example of a chemical reaction?

   A. An iron nail rusts.

   B. Butter melts in a hot pan.

   C. Clay is molded into a sculpture.

   D. Rubbing alcohol evaporates from skin.

Test-Taking Tip

When trying to determine the correct answer to a multiple-choice question, begin by deciding the correct answer before looking at the answer choices. Then, match the answer you believe to be correct with one of the possible choices.

How Are Chemical Reactions Represented?

Chemical reactions can be described in words or through symbols in a balanced chemical equation.

Directions: Use the passage to answer questions 3–5.

A chemical equation is similar to a mathematical sentence. It consists of chemical symbols that represent elements and molecules. It includes abbreviations to indicate the state of matter, and it includes numbers in the form of coefficients and subscripts. Understanding the difference between a subscript and a coefficient is essential to balancing equations. A subscript is a number that indicates the number of atoms of an element in a molecule. For example, the 2 in H_2O is a subscript that shows that a molecule of water contains two hydrogen atoms. A coefficient is a number written before a chemical symbol or formula. It indicates the number of atoms or molecules taking place in a reaction. A coefficient can be changed in order to balance an equation, but a subscript cannot.

3. What is the central idea of the paragraph?

   A. Chemical equations must be balanced because of the law of conservation of mass.

   B. Coefficients are used to balanced equations, but subscripts must remain the same.

   C. Chemical reactions can be represented by chemical equations.

   D. Chemical symbols can be used to represent elements and molecules.

4. In the chemical equation for photosynthesis shown below, _____ molecules of water enter into the reaction.

   $$6CO_2 + 6H_2O \rightarrow 6C_6H_{12}O_6 + 6O_2$$

5. The chemical equation below represents the equation in which aluminum and oxygen react to form aluminum oxide. Which statement about the chemical equation is true?

   $$4Al + 3O_2 \rightarrow 2Al_2O_3$$

   A. The subscript for aluminum in the reactants is 4.

   B. There are 2 atoms of oxygen in the reactants.

   C. There are 6 atoms of oxygen in the products.

   D. There are 7 molecules of aluminum oxide formed.

Directions: Answer the questions below.

6. Circle the equation that is balanced.

   $$3CuCl_2 + Al \rightarrow AlCl_3 + 3Cu$$

   $$2CH_4 + 4O_2 \rightarrow 2CO_2 + 4H_2O$$

   $$2Zn + 2HCl \rightarrow 2ZnCl_2 + 2H_2$$

   $$6CO_2 + 3H_2O \rightarrow C_6H_{12}O_6 + 3O_2$$

7. Hydrogen peroxide, H_2O_2, reacts to produce water, H_2O, and oxygen, O_2. Write a balanced equation for this reaction.

   _____

Energy Changes in Chemical Reactions

Exothermic reactions release energy, whereas endothermic reactions absorb energy.

Directions: Use the diagram to answer questions 8–9.

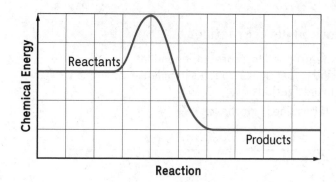

8. Which of the following processes might be represented by the diagram?

    A. A plant uses carbon dioxide, water, and energy to produce glucose and oxygen.

    B. An ice cube melting into a puddle of water.

    C. Water in a beaker on a hot plate is brought to a boil.

    D. An animal uses glucose and oxygen to release energy, water, and carbon dioxide.

9. Based on the energy change shown, the graph represents an _____ chemical reaction. Explain how you made your choice and how you know if a reaction is endothermic or exothermic.

_____

_____

_____

Chemical Reaction Rate

The rate of a chemical reaction depends on several factors, including the temperature and concentration of the substances involved.

Directions: Use the diagram to answer questions 10–11.

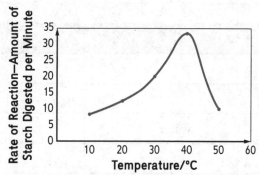

10. Which conclusion is best supported by the data?

    A. The reaction rate decreases as the temperature is increases.

    B. The reaction rate increases to some maximum, and then decreases as temperature increases.

    C. The reaction rate is independent of any changes in temperature.

    D. The reaction rate increases as temperature increases.

11. The student places starch in a Petri dish with saliva and measures the rate at which the starch is changed into sugar. The student begins at 0°C and slowly raises the temperature to 30°C over the course of 30 minutes. What error does the student make that will lead to an incorrect conclusion, and how can the error be corrected?

_____

_____

_____

This lesson will help you practice working with concepts related to the composition and formation of solutions and of acids and bases. Use it with core lesson 7.4 Solutions to reinforce and apply your knowledge.

Key Concept	Core Skills & Practices
A solution forms when one or more pure substances dissolve in another pure substance. A solution can be a gas, a liquid, or a solid.	• Identify and Interpret Independent and Dependent Variables in Scientific Investigations • Determine Hypotheses

Nature of Solutions

A solution is a mixture in which one or more substances are distributed completely and uniformly throughout another substance. The dissolved substance is called the solute, while the dissolving substance is called the solvent.

Directions: Answer the questions below.

1. Sort the given substances into solutes, solvents, or solutions. Complete the missing information in the chart by listing each substance in the correct space in the table.

club soda	detergent	oxygen	water

copper	nitrogen	soap	zinc

Solute	Solvent	Solution
carbon dioxide		
		brass
	water	
		air

2. Fish breathe oxygen that is dissolved in water. What type of solution is this?

   A. gas dissolved in gas

   B. gas dissolved in liquid

   C. solid dissolved in liquid

   D. liquid dissolved in liquid

✓ **Test-Taking Tip**

When completing a drag-and-drop activity, first check to see which information you recall, and then sort the parts of that known piece of information first. This will shorten the list and make it easier for you to sort the remaining pieces of information, especially if a logical pattern begins to appear.

The Solution Process and Solubility

How easily and quickly a solute dissolves in a solvent to form a solution depends on factors such as solute surface area, solvent temperature, the molecular structure of both substances, and the concentration of solute in a given solvent.

Directions: Answer the question below.

3. Suppose you wish to test the hypothesis "The rate at which a solute dissolves increases with the temperature of solvent." Which experiment would best allow you to do so?

   A. Dissolve identical amounts of solute in equal amounts of solvent, and measure the temperature of the resulting solutions.

   B. Dissolve excess amounts of solute in equal amounts of solvent at different temperatures, and measure how much solute does not dissolve.

   C. Raise the temperature of a quantity of solvent, and add measured amounts of solute until no more will dissolve at that temperature.

   D. Place a fixed amount of solute in a quantity of solvent, raise the solvent's temperature until all of the solute has dissolved, then measure the temperature.

Directions: Use the graph below to answer questions 4–5.

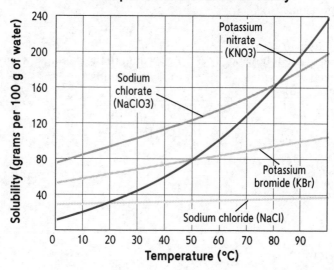

Temperature Effects on Solubility

4. In the graph above, _____ is the independent variable, and _____ is the dependent variable.

5. Suppose you mix an aqueous solution of potassium bromide (KBr) at 90°C. How many grams of KBr will dissolve in 100 g of water to produce a saturated solution?

   A. 60 g

   B. 80 g

   C. 100 g

   D. 120 g

Acids and Bases

Acids are substances that, in aqueous solutions, typically increase the hydrogen ion (H+) concentration. Bases are substances that, in aqueous solutions, increase the concentration of hydroxide (OH−) ions.

Directions: Use the reading passage below to answer questions 6–8.

A variety of acids, both weak and strong, can be found in the human body. Your body actually does a remarkable job in controlling its own pH balance. Your blood, for example, needs to remain within the range of 7.35 and 7.45. If your blood is more acidic, you suffer acidosis. If it is more basic, you are said to have alkalosis.

The body opposes the change in pH by natural chemical balancers called buffers. A buffer solution has both a weak acid (that is, an acid that does not dissociate completely) and its conjugate base in equal amounts. The liquid portion of blood is an example of a buffer solution. Among the important weak acids in the blood buffer system are carbonic acid (H_2CO_3) and phosphoric acid (H_3PO_4).

Another case in which the body generates too much acid is when someone experiences the condition called "heartburn." This occurs when too much hydrochloric acid (HCl), the strong acid generated by the stomach, is produced. This condition can be temporarily relieved by taking an antacid, which typically consists of a weak base such as sodium bicarbonate ($NaHCO_3$), to neutralize the excess stomach acid.

6. Under normal conditions, the pH of blood is slightly _____ than that of water. This makes blood _____ basic than water. Even in a severe case of _____ when the pH of blood is 7.15, water is, by comparison, a(n) _____.

7. According to the passage, which of the following is an example of an acid produced within the human body that completely dissociates?

    A. carbonic acid

    B. phosphoric acid

    C. hydrochloric acid

    D. sodium bicarbonate

8. According to the passage, which value would indicate alkalosis?

    A. 7.55

    B. 7.45

    C. 7.35

    D. 7.25

Directions: Answer the question below.

9. The value of pH is obtained from an equation based on the concentration of hydrogen ions in an aqueous solution. By taking 10 to the power of negative pH, the H^+ concentration can be determined.

$$\text{concentration of } H^+ \text{ ions} = [H^+] = 10^{-pH}$$

By using the logarithmic function, pH can be written in terms of H^+ ion concentration.

$$pH = -\log (\text{concentration of } H^+ \text{ ions}) = -\log [H^+]$$

The "concentration of H^+ ions" is written as "$[H^+]$." For this function, what are the independent and dependent variables, respectively?

    A. pH, −log

    B. $[H^+]$, pH

    C. pH, $[H^+]$

    D. −log, H^+

This lesson will help you practice working with concepts related to Earth's atmosphere. Use it with core lesson 8.1 The Atmosphere to reinforce and apply your knowledge.

Key Concept

The characteristics of the atmosphere make life on Earth possible. Changes in the types and amounts of gases in the atmosphere cause climate change, which affects organisms.

Core Skills & Practices

- Describe Data Sets Statistically
- Interpret Graphs

The Composition of the Atmosphere

The atmosphere provides gases that are necessary for life. These gases help regulate the energy from the Sun so that life on Earth can be sustained.

Directions: Answer the questions below.

1. Which characteristic of the atmosphere is **most** critical to support human survival?

   A. The atmosphere is divided into five separate layers, each with a role in dispersing energy to Earth's surface.

   B. The atmosphere provides a stable environment with oxygen and nitrogen necessary to sustain life on Earth.

   C. The atmosphere plays a key role in the evaporation and condensation of water vapor in the water cycle.

   D. The atmosphere both absorbs and reflects the Sun's energy in the form of solar radiation.

2. Which of the following would help solve the potential problem known as global warming?

   A. return to cooking on wood stoves

   B. eliminate the use of alternative energy generators

   C. reduce our dependence on all forms of fossil fuels

   D. restrict the use of solar panels on homes

Directions: Use the graph below to answer the question.

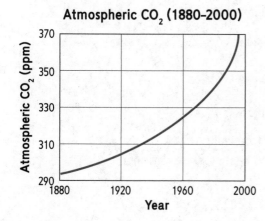

Atmospheric CO_2 (1880–2000)

3. The graph shown here recently appeared in an article that discussed the greenhouse effect (the warming of Earth's atmosphere due to atmospheric gases) on Earth. One of these gases is carbon dioxide (CO_2). What information does the author give readers in this graph?

   A. Atmospheric CO_2 increased steadily between 1880 and 2000.

   B. No measurements of atmospheric CO_2 were made after 2000.

   C. Atmospheric CO_2 levels are now less than they were in 2000.

   D. All atmospheric CO_2 should be considered harmful to human health.

The Layers of the Atmosphere

Earth's atmosphere is organized into five layers, each with a role to play in sustaining life.

Directions: Use the passage below to answer questions 4–5.

Ozone (O_3) is a gas formed by the addition of a third oxygen atom to an oxygen molecule (O_2). The formation of ozone starts when ultraviolet radiation from the Sun strikes a molecule of O_2 and splits it into two atoms of oxygen (O). Each of these atoms then bonds with other molecules of O_2 creating ozone (O_3). Ozone, in turn, can absorb additional ultraviolet radiation and split back into O_2 and O. The oxygen atom then reacts with O_2 to form O_3 again.

This cycle continuously creates ozone in the stratosphere. It also absorbs 97–99 percent of the ultraviolet radiation from the Sun before it reaches Earth's surface. If ozone did not absorb some of this radiation before it reached Earth's surface, many organisms, including humans, could not tolerate exposure to the Sun for very long. Chemicals produced by human activities destroy the ozone molecules in the stratosphere. Efforts to reduce emissions of these chemicals have been under way since 1989. As a result, the levels of ozone in the stratosphere are slowly recovering.

4. Which of these statements describes the major function of ozone in the stratosphere?

A. The ozone layer reduces the effects of pollution on Earth's breathable air.

B. The ozone layer absorbs 97–99 percent of ultraviolet radiation before it reaches Earth.

C. The ozone layer increases the effects of harmful global warming in Earth's polar regions.

D. The ozone layer decreases the presence of carbon dioxide by bonding with oxygen in CO_2 molecules.

5. What is ultraviolet radiation?

A. a band of the atmosphere with little oxygen

B. energy used to cook food in a microwave oven

C. energy that makes the purple segment of a rainbow

D. energy from the sun that can be harmful to humans

Directions: Answer the following question.

6. The ionosphere is found within the thermosphere and is composed of ions and charged particles formed by ultraviolet radiation from the Sun. Why would it be unlikely for such a layer to exist in the troposphere?

A. The temperatures are too low in the troposphere.

B. The temperatures are too high in the troposphere.

C. Too much ultraviolet radiation from the Sun reaches the troposphere.

D. Most of the ultraviolet radiation from the Sun does not reach the troposphere.

✔ Test-Taking Tip

When trying to determine the correct answer to a multiple-choice question, think about the answer before looking at the answer choices. Then, match the answer you believe to be correct with one of the possible choices.

Energy in Earth's Atmosphere

All life depends on a delicate balance of factors maintained by Earth's atmosphere. Without that balance, life on the planet could not exist.

Directions: Use the diagram to answer questions 7–8.

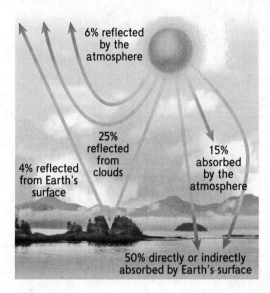

6% reflected by the atmosphere

25% reflected from clouds

15% absorbed by the atmosphere

4% reflected from Earth's surface

50% directly or indirectly absorbed by Earth's surface

7. Which of these conclusions can be inferred from the information provided in the illustration?

   A. Earth's landmasses reflect more of the Sun's energy than Earth's water.

   B. Energy reflected from Earth equals 50 percent of the Sun's energy.

   C. Earth's land and surface water absorb the Sun's energy.

   D. The atmosphere absorbs twice as much of the Sun's energy as it reflects.

8. Earth's atmosphere and surface absorb _____ percent of the Sun's energy.

Climate

Climate refers to long-term weather conditions in a particular area. There are many factors that affect climate changes.

Directions: Answer the questions below.

9. A group of scientists analyzes weather patterns from various regions of Earth. They review data from a period of several hundred years and conclude that the changes in weather experienced at the beginning of the 21st century may be the result of what phenomenon?

   A. typhoons in the North Pacific Ocean

   B. a prolonged drought season in Africa

   C. an era of glacial build-up at both poles

   D. a period of significant global warming

10. A catastrophic volcanic eruption sends a massive ash cloud into the atmosphere. The ash cloud spreads around Earth, creating a band from 40°N latitude to 30°S latitude. The cloud takes three years to disperse, and the energy balance of Earth is not maintained. Predict what might happen if such an event were to occur. Explain your reasoning.

   _____

   _____

   _____

   _____

   _____

   _____

   _____

This lesson will help you practice working with concepts related to Earth's oceans and how they affect animal and plant life, and climate. Use it with core lesson 8.2 The Oceans to reinforce and apply your knowledge.

Key Concept

Oceans have a great impact on Earth's climate and organisms. The movement and characteristics of oceans differ with depth and distance from the equator.

Core Skills & Practice

- Identify and Interpret Independent and Dependent Variables in Scientific Investigations
- Apply Scientific Models

Water on Earth

The sources and properties of oceans, seas, lakes, and rivers affect both the climate and organisms that live on Earth.

Directions: Use the diagram below to answer questions 1–2.

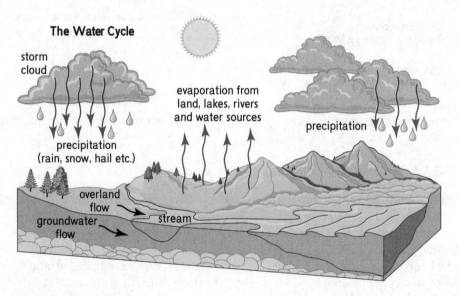

1. According to the diagram, which of the following would be the best definition of the label **precipitation**?

   A. moisture that falls to Earth

   B. the gases that surround Earth

   C. the seeping of water into Earth

   D. moisture that evaporates into the sky

2. Based on the diagram, which statement summarizes the primary function of the water cycle?

   A. the formation of storm clouds over a stream and land at the same time

   B. the evaporation of water from land and streams due to energy

   C. the back-and-forth movement of water between Earth's surface and atmosphere

   D. the removal of fresh water from land by the actions of both runoff and the growth of vegetation

The World's Oceans

The Pacific Ocean, the Atlantic Ocean, and the Indian Ocean are the three major oceans on Earth. Two smaller oceans, the Arctic Ocean and the Southern Ocean, are located near Earth's poles. All the oceans are interconnected and thus form one global ocean.

Directions: Use the table below to answer questions 3–4.

A scientist tested the salinity of water samples at four locations along 161 km of coast. She sampled from next to a glacier at the water's edge, off a barrier island, in an estuary, and in water 3 km from shore. The table shows the results of the tests.

Sample	February Test	April Test	June Test	August Test
Sample 1	37 ppt	36 ppt	37 ppt	37 ppt
Sample 2	36 ppt	34 ppt	33 ppt	32 ppt
Sample 3	32 ppt	32 ppt	32 ppt	32 ppt
Sample 4	36 ppt	37 ppt	37 ppt	37 ppt

3. What do the data from the experiment show?

A. Samples 2 and 4 show decreasing salinity levels.

B. Samples 1 and 2 have stable salinity levels.

C. Samples 1 and 3 show the lowest solubility rates for the salt dissolving in the water.

D. Samples 2 and 3 indicate a mixture of fresh water with salt water.

4. In this scenario, the salinity of the water is the _____ variable and the location along the coast is the _____ variable.

Directions: Answer the questions below.

5. High tides occur on the side of Earth nearest the Moon and on the side of Earth farthest from the Moon. Low ocean tides occur on each side of Earth between the positions of the high tides. What can you infer causes the high tide that is on the side of Earth closest to the Moon?

A. Earth's gravity

B. the Moon's gravity

C. the rotation of Earth

D. the rotation of the Moon

6. A scientist does an experiment testing ocean water from various depths in the ocean. He wants to find the correlation between the variables of temperature and density. He tests water from the ocean surface (Sample A), then every 100 m, with his last sample (Sample K) taken from 1,000 m below the surface. What should the scientist find is the difference between Sample A and Sample K?

A. Sample A is denser and has a lower temperature than Sample K.

B. Sample A is denser and has a higher temperature than Sample K.

C. Sample A is less dense and has a lower temperature than Sample K.

D. Sample A is less dense and has a higher temperature than Sample K.

Impact of Oceans

Directions: Use the passage below to answer questions 7–8.

Water transmits much of the light that strikes it. To *transmit* means "to allow to pass through." This explains why it is easy to see through a thin layer of water. However, it gets harder to see through water that is deeper, because water does not transmit light completely. It always absorbs some light. When sunlight travels down from the ocean surface, more of that light is absorbed as the depth increases. Little or no light reaches the ocean's deepest parts.

The distribution of light affects both the temperature of ocean waters and the ocean's living things. Ocean surface temperatures range from –2° C near the poles to 30° C near the equator. Yet, throughout the ocean, temperature decreases with depth. Even in the tropics, the deepest ocean water is always cold. Little light reaches these depths to heat the water.

7. What can you conclude about ocean life, based on the passage?

    A. Plants that depend on photosynthesis to survive live in the upper layer of the ocean.

    B. Creatures that live near the ocean floor along the coastline live in complete darkness.

    C. Fish that live in the deepest oceans depend completely on their sense of smell to find food.

    D. The same species that live near the ocean surface at the equator also live near the poles.

8. Explain how life in shallow regions of the ocean would be different than life in the deep ocean?

    _____

    _____

    _____

    _____

✅ Test-Taking Tip

When you read a passage during a test, you need to eliminate information that is not necessary for answering questions. One way to do this is to read the passage, taking notes of important information, and then reviewing the questions to see what information is covered and what is not.

9. Many outside influences affect the makeup of the oceans. Categorize the following influences by writing each term in the appropriate box.

| overfishing | glacial meltwater | surface evaporation | coral bleaching |

| water pollution | global warming | ebb tides |

Human Influences	Natural Influences

This lesson will help you practice working with concepts related to Earth's structure, composition, and landforms. Use it with core lesson 8.3 Earth's Structure, Composition, and Landforms to reinforce and apply your knowledge.

Key Concept

Earth is divided into three layers with different compositions. Interactions between Earth's tectonic plates cause most of Earth's volcanoes, earthquakes, and mountains. Minerals, rocks, and soil can be formed or changed during the rock cycle.

Core Skills & Practices

- Understand and Apply Scientific Models, Theories, and Processes
- Draw Conclusions

Earth's Structure

Earth is divided into three layers. The core lies at the center; the crust is the outer layer. The mantle fills the area between the core and the crust.

Directions: Use the image below to answer questions 1–3.

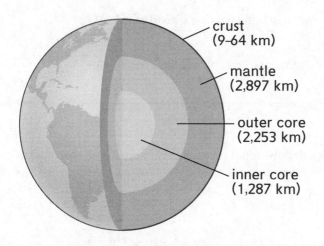

crust
(9–64 km)

mantle
(2,897 km)

outer core
(2,253 km)

inner core
(1,287 km)

1. Which of Earth's layers or sub-layers is the thickest?

   A. crust

   B. mantle

   C. inner core

   D. outer core

2. According to the image, the crust varies in thickness. Which of the following explains the differences in thickness?

   A. Continental crust varies in thickness because of valleys, plains, plateaus, and mountain ranges.

   B. The crust under oceans is always 9.6 km thick in the Pacific Ocean and slightly thicker under the Atlantic Ocean.

   C. The difference in thickness is related to the equator, with Earth's crust thicker at the equator and thinner at the poles.

   D. Earth is not perfectly round, and the crust is thinnest at the narrowest part of the planet.

3. Which is the most accurate comparison to Earth's structure?

   A. Earth is most like an onion with many layers of even thickness.

   B. Earth is most like a basketball with a bumpy surface and a hollow center.

   C. Earth is most like a golf ball with a hard center, a thick middle, and a thin uneven surface.

   D. Earth is most like a walnut with an uneven center and a hard outer shell.

Directions: Use the passage below to answer questions 4–5.

A liquid such as water has different physical properties from a solid such as ice. Earth's layers also have different physical properties. Scientists recognize five layers of Earth based on their physical properties. Two of those layers are discussed here.

The rigid, relatively cool outer layer of Earth is called the lithosphere. The lithosphere is made up of the crust and the solid portion of the upper mantle. The lithosphere is brittle, meaning that it can crack and break. When it does crack, large amounts of force are released. These forces can cause earthquakes. Cracks in the lithosphere can also allow hot material from deeper inside Earth to rise to the surface. Because the lithosphere is the outer layer of Earth, it is the layer that we know the most about.

The hot layer underneath the lithosphere is the asthenosphere. The asthenosphere is the part of the upper mantle that can slowly flow. Even though it can flow, the asthenosphere is actually a solid.

4. Students are asked to make models of the lithosphere. Which of these models accurately depicts the lithosphere?

   A. a grainy, lumpy sphere made of multi-colored clay

   B. a slick, rounded ball made of rubber

   C. a flat, smooth surface made of molded plastic

   D. an uneven, cracked surface made of plaster

5. Which of these definitions of **mantle** shows the correct use in this context?

   A. a solid framework

   B. a layer of Earth between the crust and the core

   C. a liquid or solid coating spread evenly over a substance

   D. anything that covers or hides completely

Earth's Composition

When Earth formed, the heaviest elements sank toward the center, and the lighter elements remained close to the surface. Iron and nickel are the main elements in the core, while the mantle is mostly iron and magnesium. The surface crust mostly consists of silica and oxygen.

Directions: Answer the question below.

6. A scientist has several rock samples, some of which may be hematite. She already has a piece of hematite that she has studied at another time. How might she go about determining which of the new samples are hematite and which are not?

_____

_____

_____

 Test-Taking Tip

When answering a short answer question, always write in complete sentences. It is often useful to reword the question into the format of an opening sentence. Then add specific information and keep to the topic. Check that all parts of your answer are directly relevant to the question you are answering.

7. Which of the following items are examples of weathering or deposition. Sort the examples into the correct categories. Write each example in the appropriate box.

| soil laid down at the mouth of a river | ice cracking the surface of a rock |

| underground water dissolving limestone | rubble left after a glacier recedes |

| a natural bridge carved by wind | rocks and soil at the base of a landslide |

Examples of Deposition	Examples of Weathering

The Theory of Plate Tectonics

Millions of years ago, Earth had only one continent, called Pangaea. That huge continent broke up and spread apart, creating continents separated by large oceans.

Directions: Use the map below to answer questions 8–10.

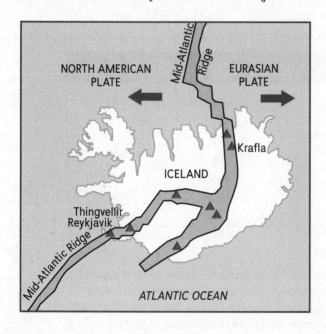

8. According to the map, the Mid-Atlantic Ridge runs between the _____ plate and the _____ plate.

9. Which statement is supported by the information in the map?

   A. The North American Plate and Eurasian Plate are moving towards each other.

   B. The North American Plate is moving over and covering the Mid-Atlantic Ridge.

   C. The spread of the Mid-Atlantic Ridge will divide Iceland into three separate islands.

   D. The nation of Iceland straddles two major tectonic plates and the Mid-Atlantic Ridge.

10. Which event is an example of something that would occur at a convergent plate boundary?

    A. the continuous build-up of lava rock that forms the string of Hawaiian Islands

    B. the ongoing movement of North and South America away from Europe and Africa

    C. the spreading sea floor and widening of the Atlantic Ocean by the Mid-Atlantic Ridge

    D. the collision of the Indian Plate and the Eurasian Plate forming the Himalaya Mountains

This lesson will help you practice working with concepts related to Earth's natural resources. Use it with core lesson 8.4 Earth's Resources to reinforce and apply your knowledge.

Key Concept	**Core Skills & Practices**
Earth supplies a wide variety of natural resources. All organisms on Earth, including humans, use resources provided by the environment. The use of resources has both advantages and disadvantages.	• Express Scientific Information or Findings Verbally • Interpret Graphics

Natural Resources

Natural resources are substances, organisms, or forms of energy that occur in nature and that are used by living things.

Directions: Answer the following questions.

1. Sort the following resources into the correct category. Write the term in the appropriate box.

coal	flowers	diamonds	gold	oxygen
oil	river water	silver	sunlight	wind

Renewable Natural Resources	Nonrenewable Natural Resources

2. A government agency organizes a research project on reducing pollution in the air and water supply. Which of these agencies would most likely conduct this type of research, given the purpose of the research?

   A. National Park Service

   B. Food and Drug Administration

   C. Environmental Protection Agency

   D. Agency for Healthcare Research and Quality

3. Based on what you have learned about natural resources, predict which factor is most likely to influence how the United States uses natural resources 100 years from today.

   A. Available stores of uranium

   B. Resource use by other countries

   C. Profits made by power companies

   D. The remaining supply of fossil fuels

Nonrenewable Energy Resources

Fossil fuels, including oil, gas, coal, and nuclear energy, are nonrenewable energy sources.

Directions: Use the graph to answer question 4.

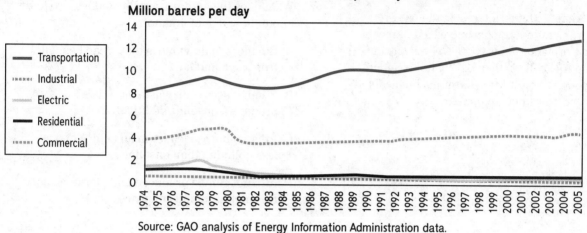

Annual U.S. Oil Consumption, by Sector, 1974–2005

Source: GAO analysis of Energy Information Administration data.

4. Based on the data above, which is a reasonable conclusion about oil use in electricity production between 1985 and 2005?

   A. Electric-power usage per person increased, but the overall expenses of purchasing oil decreased each year.

   B. Electric-power usage did not increase during this 20-year period, because the US population did not increase during that time.

   C. Electric-power production using oil remained consistent, implying that increased power production came from other resources.

   D. Methods for producing electric power became more efficient, so the use of oil to produce electricity decreased dramatically.

Directions: Answer the following questions.

5. Which statement best compares the hazards of using nuclear energy to energy produced by a coal-burning power plant?

   A. Both produce waste that threatens the health of living things.

   B. Both use nuclear fission as a process to create electrical energy.

   C. Both use a steam-driven turbine to turn an electric generator.

   D. Both create carbon dioxide and release the gas into the atmosphere.

6. How does burning fossil fuels affect Earth's atmosphere and change its climate?

   _____

   _____

   _____

 **Test-Taking Tip**

A short-answer test question may have two or more related topics. When answering a short-answer question that has more than one part, separate the parts of the question. As you write your answer, mentally check off each part to ensure that you provide a complete answer.

Renewable Energy Resources

Nature provides a number of resources that provide energy and promote sustainability. The Sun, wind, moving water, and heat sources beneath Earth's surface are all renewable energy sources.

Directions: Use the information to answer question 7.

In the United States, interest in the use of field crops for energy has increased in recent years. Corn and grains can also be made into a liquid fuel called ethanol. Ethanol is added to gasoline to reduce the harmful chemicals produced by running engines.

7. What does the author want the audience to know about the value of ethanol?

   A. Ethanol's main value is that it can be made from corn and hay.

   B. Ethanol uses crop waste materials to produce a gasoline additive.

   C. Ethanol burns cleaner in an engine and is less polluting than gasoline.

   D. Ethanol can be produced and marketed as fuel in developing countries.

Directions: Use the map to answer questions 8–9.

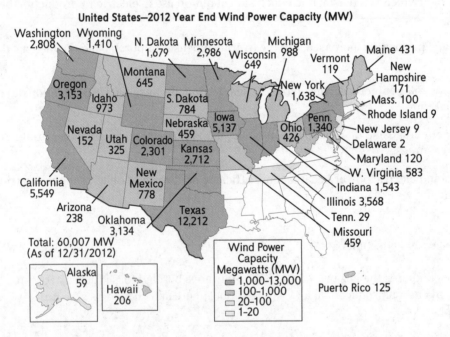

United States—2012 Year End Wind Power Capacity (MW)

8. Which statement is supported by the data in the map?

   A. States on the West Coast of the US have greater wind resources than other states.

   B. No eastern US states produce more than 250 megawatts of wind-power energy.

   C. States with no wind-power generators generate sufficient hydroelectric energy.

   D. Texas and California have invested heavily in using wind-power technology.

9. Which conclusion can be drawn from the map?

   A. States in the Midwest generate more wind-power energy than eastern states.

   B. Utah, Rhode Island, and Michigan will increase their use wind-power technology.

   C. All western states have embraced the technology needed to generate wind-power energy.

   D. New York and Pennsylvania have more wind available for power generation than Nebraska.

This lesson will help you practice working with concepts related to the interactions between Earth's systems. Use it with core lesson 8.5 Interactions Between Earth's Systems to reinforce and apply your knowledge.

Key Concept

Earth's systems interact, resulting in a variety of effects, some of which are disastrous.

Core Skills & Practices

- Use Sampling Techniques to Answer Scientific Questions.
- Follow a Multistep Procedure

Weather

Weather, the condition of the atmosphere at a particular place and time, is a daily concern worldwide.

Directions: Use the passage below to answer the question below.

> The study of weather is the study of the changes that take place in Earth's atmosphere, the layer of gases that surrounds the planet. A local weather report usually includes the following four features:
>
> - **Temperature** is a measure of the warmth of the air.
>
> - **Humidity** is a measure of the water vapor in the air. Humidity readings are usually given as percentages. A humidity reading of 90 percent means that the air contains 90 percent of the water vapor it can possibly hold at that particular temperature.
>
> - **Wind** refers to air movement. Both the speed and direction of the wind are usually cited. Wind direction refers to the direction from which the wind is blowing.
>
> - **Air pressure** (**barometric pressure**) refers to the weight of the atmosphere. Air pressure depends on atmospheric temperature, humidity, and air movement. A high-pressure reading usually indicates clear, pleasant weather. A low-pressure reading indicates wet or stormy weather.

1. By analyzing weather data, meteorologists can predict weather patterns that affect people several days later. Select the type of weather data that corresponds to each weather occurrence from the choices provided. Write the type of weather data in the appropriate space in the table.

high barometric pressure		high humidity
temperature		heavy winds

Type of Weather Data	Weather Occurrence
	Tropical rain storms
	A heat wave
	Clear, pleasant weather
	Broken tree branches and falling limbs

Earth's Changing Surface

Changes occur on Earth's surface all the time. Slow changes may result from weathering or erosion. Rapid, more violent changes can result from events such as earthquakes or volcanic eruptions.

Directions: Answer the questions below.

2. A class goes to visit a beach. On the dunes at the back of the beach, the sand lies in a rippled pattern. High tides have never reached this far up on the beach. What is the main process that created the rippled pattern on the beach?

   A. wind erosion

   B. gravity erosion

   C. physical weathering

   D. chemical weathering

3. Agriculture frequently contributes to soil erosion. Farmers want to prevent soil erosion but using positive conservation practices. Which of these agricultural activities *decreases* soil erosion?

   A. plowing up land and leaving the acreage unplanted

   B. using farm land for building houses, businesses, and roads

   C. planting a row of cottonwood trees and low-cover shrubs at the edge of fields

   D. introducing a herd of cattle that eats all the native vegetation

 Test-Taking Tip

When answering a multiple-choice question that includes a scenario, look for typographic clues to help find the right answer. Italicized, underlined, and boldfaced words give you a hint about which answer is correct.

Directions: Use the diagram below to answer questions 4–5.

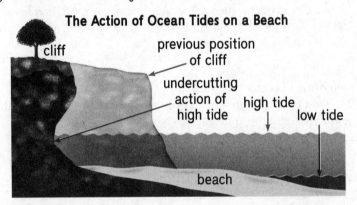

The Action of Ocean Tides on a Beach

4. A scientist studies the profile of a beach that has extremely high tides. The scientist notes how the cliff face changes over several seasons. What two processes does the scientist discover are acting on the beach and cliff?

   A. wind erosion and gravity erosion

   B. wind erosion and physical weathering

   C. water erosion and physical weathering

   D. water erosion and chemical weathering

5. What is one result of the action of the high tide waves on the cliff?

   A. a decrease in the amount of beach

   B. an increase in the amount of beach

   C. a decrease in the height of the cliff

   D. an increase in the height of the tide

Extreme Weather Systems

Hurricanes, tornados, and powerful thunderstorms are hazards caused by extreme weather patterns.

Directions: Use the chart below to answer questions 6–7.

Category	Wind Speed (mph)	Damage at Landfall	Storm Surge (feet)
1	74–95	Minimal	4–5
2	96–110	Moderate	6–8
3	111–130	Extensive	9–12
4	131–155	Extreme	13–18
5	Over 155	Catastrophic	19+

6. A hurricane strikes the coast of the Bahamas and moves westward toward the United States. When it strikes the Bahamas, the hurricane is a Category 2. Forecasters predict that it will become a Category 4 by the time it reaches the United States. Explain the difference between the storm that strikes the Bahamas and the one that strikes the United States.

_____

_____

_____

_____

7. A storm begins off the coast of Africa. The storm quickly becomes a Category 3 hurricane. After the hurricane strikes land, it loses energy. The wind speed of the hurricane is reduced to 85 miles per hour. What type of hurricane is it at this point?

A. Category 1

B. Category 2

C. Category 3

D. Category 4

Directions: Answer the questions below.

8. What is the relationship between a tornado and a thunderstorm?

A. Rapidly rotating air masses collide and form a tornado, and if the tornado is large enough, it generates a thunderstorm.

B. When a thunderstorm lifts rotating air near the ground from a horizontal to vertical position, a tornado may occur.

C. High winds from opposite directions meet near a thunderstorm, creating a funnel that drops out of the sky to become a tornado.

D. When massive thunderclouds revolve in the air, they create a funnel effect, which may become a tornado.

9. Which of these conditions is necessary for a storm to become a hurricane?

A. wind and light rain on a hot day

B. a large thunderstorm colliding with dry winds

C. wind, rain, and a cold front from the north

D. thunderstorms moving over warm tropical ocean water

This lesson will help you practice working with concepts related to structures in the universe. Use it with core lesson 9.1 Structures in the Universe to reinforce and apply your knowledge.

Key Concept

The universe is billions of years old and contains stars, solar systems, galaxies, and all the matter that exists within them.

Core Skills & Practices

- Identify the Strengths and Weaknesses of One or More Experimental Designs
- Analyze Structures

The Universe

The Universe consists of everything that exists throughout space, from our sun and solar system, to galaxies, stars, matter, and energy.

Directions: Use the timeline below to answer questions 1–2.

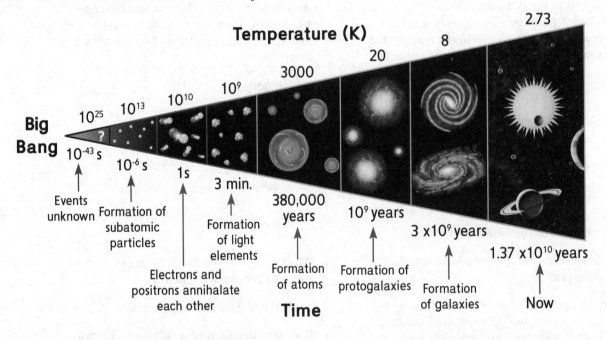

1. According to the timeline, which statement is true?

   A. All events that occurred three minutes after the Big Bang have been proven true.

   B. The development of protogalaxies took much longer than the formation of atoms.

   C. The matter that formed stars and planets did not exist until 1.37×10^{10} years passed.

   D. The Big Bang theory holds that the temperature of the universe has decreased over time.

2. Which of these events occurred when the universe was 3 billion years old?

   A. Earth formed

   B. atoms formed

   C. galaxies formed

   D. elements formed

Directions: Answer the questions below.

3. Place the sequence of events in the life cycle of a star in the correct order. Write the phrases in the appropriate numbered box below.

| red giant | fusion | protostar | nebula | white dwarf |

1.	2.	3.	4.	5.

The Stars

Stars appear to be small lights in the night sky, but they are actually hot, burning balls of gases that generate heat and light. Stars are categorized according to mass, temperature, age, diameter, and the amount of light they give off.

Directions: Answer the questions below.

4. Which of these is a direct result of a supernova?

   A. development into a white dwarf

   B. complete destruction of a galaxy

   C. production of heavy, metallic elements

   D. formation of a recognizable star pattern in the sky

5. Every star in every galaxy in the universe is a source of energy. Within each star, including the Sun, nuclear energy heats the star and keeps it from collapsing due to the force of gravity. Meanwhile, each star's own energy and the _____ between the star and other stars work together to keep the star within a path inside its own galaxy.

6. Which statement accurately expresses the nature of a protostar?

   A. A protostar is a star that has gone supernova.

   B. Protostars have a ball-like center and a disk that remains stationary in space.

   C. The spherical and glowing center that forms in a nebula, is a protostar.

   D. All protostars will eventually develop into red giants.

7. A black hole is the collapsed leftovers of a supernova. Some scientists believe a black hole is like a strong funnel that may pull in material from nearby stars. Not even light can escape from a black hole. Which of these common items most resembles the actions of a black hole?

   A. a blizzard

   B. an iceberg

   C. a waterfall

   D. a whirlpool

 Test-Taking Tip

When answering fill-in-the-blank questions, always review the answer before handing in your test. Fill-in-the-blank questions form complete sentences. Does your answer sound like a complete sentence? If not, revise the answer to make a logical sentence.

Types of Galaxies

A galaxy is composed of stars, dust, and gases that are held together by gravity. All galaxies are large and contain from a few million to more than a trillion stars.

Directions: Answer the questions below.

8. Choose the option that correctly completes each sentence.

Galaxies are groups of stars, dust and gas that are held together by **1** Select . . . ▼ . Most galaxies are **2** Select . . . ▼ galaxies with arms that spin out from a center core. Our own galaxy is called **3** Select . . . ▼ . Our galaxy has many other suns with planets. Our own Sun is only one of more than 100 billion **4** Select . . . ▼ .

1 Select . . . ▼

A. mass

B. motion

C. gravity

D. electrical charge

2 Select . . . ▼

A. spiral

B. quasar

C. irregular

D. elliptical

3 Select . . . ▼

A. Tarantula

B. Andromeda

C. the Big Dipper

D. the Milky Way

4 Select . . . ▼

A. stars

B. nebula

C. planets

D. comets

9. A proposal is made to send rockets carrying telescopes, cameras, and data sensors into space. The plan calls for the rockets to be launched in different directions to gather information that would give scientists a more complete picture of the Milky Way and enable them to fully map all of its stars and orbiting planets. What obstacles make such a project impractical?

_____

_____

_____

_____

10. Which of these properties is common to planets, stars, and galaxies?

A. They radiate light.

B. They have gravity.

C. They give off intense heat.

D. They are spherical in shape.

This lesson will help you practice working with concepts related to Earth's solar system. Use it with core lesson 9.2 Structures in the Solar System to reinforce and apply your knowledge.

Key Concept

Earth is part of a solar system and interacts with other parts of its solar system.

Core Skills & Practices

- Cite Specific Textual Evidence to Support a Finding or Conclusion
- Use Ratio and Rate Reasoning

Earth's Solar System

Our solar system consists of eight planets, their moons, and other objects that orbit the Sun.

Directions: Use the table to answer questions 1–2.

Planet	Distance from Sun (AU)	Orbital Period (Earth Years)	Period of Rotation (Earth Days)	Mass (Earth = 1)
Venus	0.72	0.62	243	0.815
Earth	1	1	1	1
Jupiter	5.20	11.86	0.41	318
Neptune	30.06	164.8	0.72	17

1. An astronomer is comparing how fast Venus, Earth, Jupiter, and Neptune each spin on their axes. Write the names of the four planets in order from slowest to fastest in the boxes provided.

Slowest 1.	2.	3.	Fastest 4.

2. Neptune is about _____ times farther away from the Sun than Jupiter.

Test-Taking Tip

When a test requires you to put steps or items in a cause-and-effect sequence, it is sometimes helpful to work backwards. Find the last item or the final result. Then work backwards from there. Find the item that caused the final result. Continue until you have all the items placed in order. Then look at the items from the first item to the last to make sure that each item would cause the next item to happen.

Directions: Use the information to answer questions 3–4.

More than 40,000 asteroids orbit the Sun between the orbits of Mars and Jupiter. Together, the mass of all the asteroids is about one-thirtieth the mass of Earth's moon. Some astronomers hypothesize that asteroids are fragments that never combined to form a planet. Others suggest that they are the remains of a planet that came apart as a result of a collision with a comet. It is possible that asteroids can be pulled out of their orbits to become moons of nearby planets. Two moons of Mars may be asteroids that were captured.

3. Write a definition of an asteroid that could be added to the beginning of the passage.

_____

_____

_____

4. Which information from the passage most directly refutes the claim that asteroids once formed a planet?

A. There are more than 40,000 asteroids.

B. The mass of all the asteroids is only a fraction of the mass of Earth's moon.

C. Most asteroids orbit the Sun between the orbits of Mars and Jupiter.

D. Asteroids can be pulled out of their orbits to become moons of nearby planets.

Earth's Movement and the Moon

Earth rotates on its axis as it revolves around the Sun, just as the Moon rotates on its axis as it revolves around Earth.

Directions: Answer the following questions.

5. Which phenomenon on Earth would change if Earth started spinning more slowly on its axis?

A. A year would be shorter.

B. Seasons would not exist.

C. A day would last longer.

D. Eclipses would not occur.

6. A location on Earth is experiencing winter. Which statement about the location is true?

A. It is at its farthest point from the Sun.

B. It is on the part of Earth tilted away from the Sun.

C. It is on the side of Earth facing away from the Sun.

D. It is being blocked from the Sun by the Moon.

7. Weight is a result of the force of gravity on a mass. The force of gravity varies among different planets and their moons. The gravitational force you would experience depends both on the mass of the object and its diameter. The force of gravity at the surface of the Moon, for example, is only one-sixth Earth's gravity. Although an object's mass would remain the same if it were brought to the Moon, its weight would change. Based on this information, what additional information would you need to calculate the weight of an astronaut on the Moon?

A. The distance to the Moon

B. The diameter of the Moon

C. The astronaut's mass on Earth

D. The astronaut's weight on Earth

Earth's Age

Earth is estimated to be approximately 4.6 billion years old, and its history is divided into segments called eons, eras, periods, and epochs.

Directions: Use the diagram to answer questions 8–9.

Potassium-40 is a radioactive isotope commonly used in radiometric dating to find the age of rocks on Earth. The process involves determining how much potassium-40 has decayed since the rock was formed. The graph represents the decay of potassium-40.

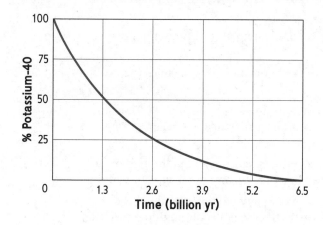

8 What percent of the original sample remains after 5.2 billion years?

A. 25 percent   C. 3.125 percent

B. 6.25 percent   D. 12.50 percent

9. Scientists select particular isotopes based on their half-life. According to the graph, the half-life of potassium-40 is _____ years. If a sample begins with 500 g of potassium-40, explain how to find the mass that remains after 2.6 billion years.

_____

_____

_____

Directions: Use the diagram to answer questions 10–11.

A group of researchers identified the layers of rock shown in the diagram. They are analyzing the layers to learn about Earth's past.

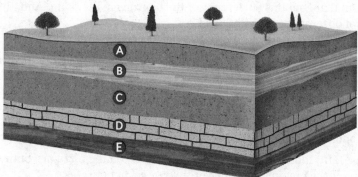

10. Which conclusion can they reach, based on the layers?

A. Layer D is the oldest layer.

B. Layer A is older than Layer B.

C. Layer C formed later than Layer E.

D. Layers B and E formed at the same time.

11. The researchers are studying fossils found in each of the rock layers. Which of the following can the researchers determine through relative dating?

A. The year in which each organism died

B. The order in which the organisms lived

C. How old each organism was when it died

D. How long it took for each organism to fossilize

Lesson 1.1

Skeletal, Muscular, and Nervous Systems, p. 2

1. **B** Each bone is composed of living, growing tissue. If a bone breaks, one type of bone cell breaks down the damaged tissue while another type of bone cell begins to rebuild the bone.

2. Bone marrow produces blood cells. The patient who receives a bone-marrow transplant would make blood from the donor's marrow. Assuming the donor's marrow makes healthy blood cells, the patient could then start making healthy blood cells.

3. **A** As people grow older, cartilage can wear down and cause bones to rub together at the knee joint. This can cause pain.

4. The knee would be able to rotate in many directions instead of bending and straightening in only one direction.

5. **C** The skeletal and muscular systems are interrelated. The muscular system uses muscles to move the bones of the skeletal system.

6. **A** Muscles that are used to control bone movement are all voluntary muscles you can consciously control. These muscles are connected to bones by **tendons**, which are bands of strong, fibrous connective tissue.

7. **A** Muscles are tissues that contract, which occurs when muscle fibers shorten and pull together. Muscles attach to bones, allowing you to walk, run, throw, dance, or do any other type of activity.

8. If the smooth muscles of the intestines were voluntary, you would have to think to direct the muscles' movement in order for food to be digested and waste to be removed. It might be possible to stay alive this way, but it would be a lot more difficult than just having a system that works without conscious control.

9. Muscles receive electrical signals from the nervous system which enables them to contract or relax.

10. Tendons connect muscles, bones, and joints. If a person had tendon damage, he or she would probably have pain and limited use of the corresponding joint.

11. **B** The axon relays the electrical message from the cell body to the terminal ends.

12. **C** The nerve pulse travels from the dendrite (C), to the cell body (B), to the axon (D), and finally to the terminal endings (E).

13. **A** The brain is a complex organ that contains 90 percent of the neurons in the body. And, different portions of the brain control different body functions.

14. The movement away from the cool surface most likely took longer than the movement away from the hot surface. The hot surface likely triggered a reflex response, which bypasses the brain and is therefore faster than other responses.

Lesson 1.2

Digestive, Excretory, Respiratory, and Circulatory Systems, p. 5

1. **D** The gallbladder helps digest fatty foods. The pepperoni and cheese on the pizza are both sources of fat. The other foods listed consist mainly of either protein or carbohydrates.

2. **C** Absorption of nutrients occurs in the small intestine.

3.

BEGINNING	mouth	esophagus	stomach	small intestine	large intestine	rectum	END

4. **A** Each nephron is surrounded by a network of capillaries that are critical to the elimination of wastes.

5. **B** Each kidney has about 1 million nephrons—the number is critical to the task of reabsorbing materials and eliminating wastes.

6. **D** Diffusion moves from high pressure to low, so at lower air pressures the gradient between inside and outside the lungs is reduced.

7. **B** Both nephrons and alveoli are tiny structures through which molecules diffuse.

8. **C** The tasks of the circulatory system are to transport and deliver nutrients, gases, and wastes throughout the body.

9. **A** A larger body requires additional oxygen and nutrients and thus more demand on the heart.

10. **D** The left pulmonary artery transports deoxygenated blood, which has a high percentage of carbon dioxide, to the lung.

11.

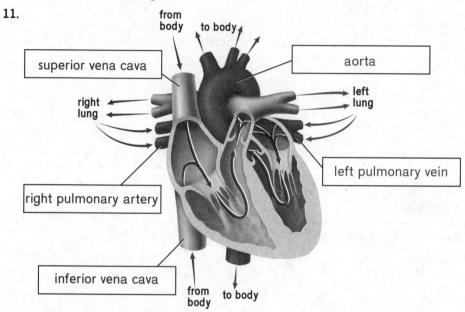

12. Blood in vessels drawn in a lighter shade, is returning from different body parts back to the heart and lungs. This blood lacks oxygen. Blood in vessels drawn in a darker has already passed through the lungs and carries oxygen.

Lesson 1.3

Endocrine and Reproductive Systems, p. 8

1. **C** The stress hormone epinephrine is released from the adrenal gland which means that pathway F is the correct answer choice.

2. The hypothalamus is the part of the brain that controls the pituitary gland, which secretes multiple hormones. These hormones, in turn, trigger body processes either directly at multiple sites, or by controlling other glands that release hormones.

3. **B** Bones, which are part of pathway C, release growth hormones. Even if you did not know this fact you could reason that bones increase in size as you grow, so the pathway including bones would be a logical choice.

4. **C** Glands in the endocrine system release chemicals called hormones which travel through the blood-stream to specific cells throughout the body where they carry out their function.

5. The structures that link the endocrine and reproductive systems are called endocrine glands.

6. **D** The fallopian tube is the pathway for an egg to travel from the ovary to he uterus in the female reproductive system, and the vas deferens is the pathway for sperm to travel outside the body in the male reproductive system.

7. **A** In males, sperm mature in the testes which descend from the lower abdominal region. They are not located in the abdomen.

8. **B** Fertilization of the egg must first occur for reproduction to begin.

9. A Because the mother's and fetus's circulatory systems are linked, substances that enter the mother's bloodstream are transported to the fetus.

10. D Because the mother's and fetus's circulatory systems are linked, waste gases are released by the mother.

11.

Hormone	Site where released	What it affects
testosterone	Testes	sperm production
Estrogen	Ovary	breast development
Progesterone	Ovary	thickening of uterine lining

Lesson 1.4

Homeostasis, p. 11

1. B The body responds to changes in blood pH by regulating the amount of carbon dioxide in the bloodstream. There is no similar stimulus-response mechanism related to the other physical characteristics listed.

2. A Mobility in the joints cannot be regulated by a stimulus-response system whereas the other examples can be regulated by such a system.

3.

1 D
2 A
3 C
4 B

4. B Because a response is triggered by a stimulus, the stimulus must always occur before the response.

5. Internal stimuli would include hunger, thirst, or a rise or drop in body temperature. Possible external stimuli could include heat, sunlight, cold, and inclement weather.

6. D The maintenance of relatively constant oxygen levels is similar to homeostasis that occurs within the human body. Homeostasis within the body involves maintaining a steady internal environment.

7. The body produces sweat in order to cool down the skin and reduce body temperature.

8. C Unlike nonliving things, living things can exhibit a homeostatic response by regulating changes in order to maintain an internal balance.

9. D Positive feedback involves acceleration of a change in the body. A fever accelerates an increase in body temperature in order to kill an invading pathogen.

10. C From the diagram one can infer that the body functions best with lower levels of blood glucose. When levels are too high, the body responds to lower the levels.

11. Releasing insulin is the body's _____response_____ to the stimulus of absorption of glucose.

12. If the body does not produce insulin, the glucose level in the blood can get dangerously _____high_____.

13. B The definition of negative feedback is a mechanism to slow or reverse changes in the body in order to maintain homeostasis.

14. The doctor would need to test the patient's fasting glucose level, then test the patient's level after ingesting glucose, and then test the patient's glucose levels at regular intervals thereafter to determine if the glucose levels are returning to normal.

Lesson 1.5

Nutrition, p. 14

1. **B** Fiber is only found in carbohydrates and is necessary for healthy body functioning. The body may not get enough fiber with a diet extremely low in carbohydrates.

2. **B** In order to receive all of the necessary amino acids, humans should consume plant and animal based proteins since many amino acids are lacking in plants.

3. **A** Saturated fats are known to raise blood cholesterol, which can lead to health problems such as heart disease.

4. **B** Minerals such as calcium and potassium are inorganic, meaning they cannot be created by plants or animals, and are essential for many metabolic functions.

5. **B** In order to determine the healthfulness of a food, it is essential to know its effects, including the health risks and benefits.

6. **B** Canola oil is lower in saturated fat than olive oil. Each of the other substitutions would increase the individual's consumption of saturated fat.

7. **C** Canola oil is the highest in polyunsaturated fat according to the graph.

8.

Lunch	Bagel	Nectarine	yogurt
Dinner	Spaghetti	salad	eggs

9. **D** Based on a 2,000 calorie diet, two servings with milk would give you 20% of your recommended daily amount of potassium.

10. **A** Consuming 2 servings of dry cereal would equal 180 calories.

11. If Jiang burns 1,800 calories per day but consumes only 1,550 calories per day, it will take him ____14 days____ to lose one pound of fat.

Lesson 1.6

Disease Prevention, p. 17

1. **D** Hepatitis is an infectious disease transmitted through the blood. Infectious diseases are caused by pathogens.

2. The sneeze spreads virus-filled saliva through the air. This airborne saliva can be breathed in by an individual, allowing the pathogen to enter and infect that person's body.

3. **D** Both infectious and non-infectious diseases disrupt the normal functioning of the body. However, invading pathogens cause infectious diseases like influenza, while non-infectious diseases like cancer are linked to behavior or genetics.

4. **B** *E. coli* is caused by a pathogen; the other diseases are not. Pathogens must be carried from one host to another. In other words, they require a vector. In this case, contaminated food is the vector.

5. Malaria and bubonic plague are classified as infectious diseases because they are caused by pathogens that invade the body and produce an infection. A pathogen must be carried from one host to another. A vector carries a pathogen from one host to another.

6. **D** Mucous membrane lines all body cavities exposed to the outside world. The membrane and associated glands secrete a sticky liquid that traps germs and other foreign particles before they can invade cells.

7. **C** When a pathogen invades the body, antigens on the walls of the pathogen trigger an immune response. White blood cells called B cells and T cells are produced. B cells produce antibodies that attach to the antigens, thereby marking the pathogen for identification and destruction by T cells.

8.

FIRST			LAST
B	A	C	D

9. **A** Syphilis is a disease passed on during sexual activity. At this time, there is no vaccine for this STD, and the only preventive measures against acquiring it are behavioral.

10. **D** *Salmonella* is a food-borne illness caused by bacteria. The pathogen will readily contaminate items, such as knives, used to prepare infected food. Washing the items thoroughly after use and before using them to prepare other food will prevent spread of the bacteria.

11. **D** Although all cases of disease listed in the chart were dramatically reduced by 1998 attributable to vaccines, only one case of diphtheria was recorded. This suggests that the vaccine was highly effective and the disease was nearly eradicated.

12. In all instances, the number of cases of each disease declined dramatically with the introduction of a vaccine. However, not all vaccines were equally effective. The vaccine for diphtheria seems to have been the most effective, as cases of the disease were reduced to 1 in 1998. The reduction in mumps is also impressive. The least effective vaccine appears to be the pertussis vaccine, where the number of cases after the vaccine remained relatively high after use of the vaccine in 1998.

Lesson 2.1

Living Things and Their Environment, p. 20

1. **B** This is the only factor listed that does not involve living things, which are considered biotic factors.

2. No, because a population by definition includes only individuals of the same species. You might find two species of lizards but they would not be part of the same population.

3. **C** In a stable ecosystem, the duck and bass populations would not change much in size.

4. Ducks and bass have similar niches in that they both eat small fishes, but their niches differ in other ways. If small fish became scarce, ducks might eat less desirable foods (insects, snails) on the edge of the pond, and bass may go to different depths and/or choose smaller fish, tadpoles, etc.

5.

Research Question	Level of Ecology Studied
How does hurricane damage in a wetland affect the food chain there?	A. ecosystem
How do birds in a flock behave to prevent predators from taking their eggs?	B. population
How does the addition of a bass to a pond affect the populations of other fish species?	C. community

6. **C** Niches are the specific roles organisms play as determined by their adaptations, in this case their means of feeding.

7. **A** This is the only true answer; plants can grow in shallow waters where light can penetrate.

8. **D** Both biomes are highly diverse and lack severe environmental conditions.

9. The labeled biome that is both coldest and driest is _____A_____.

10. **B** Tundra is dry and temperate rain forest is wet; the other sequences are incorrect.

11. **D** Desert has highest temperatures and lowest amounts of precipitation.

Lesson 2.2

Energy Flow and Cycles of Matter, p. 23

1. **B** Producers are the base of food webs in all ecosystems.

2. **D** The role of decomposers is to release nutrients as they sustain themselves on dead matter.

3. **D** The grasshopper is a first-order heterotrophs because it eats producers.

4.   A food web could show many other examples of producers besides lettuce, such as radishes, celery, or other crop plants. It could also show other producers that the grasshopper consumes or that are eaten by other consumers in the community. It may also show that consumers other than the mouse feed on grasshoppers, and that consumers other than the hawk feed on mice. A food web would show whether any of the consumers within the community are omnivores or feed at more than one trophic level.

5. A   Mountain lions are secondary consumers. When ranchers reduced the population of mountain lions, they reduced the population of secondary consumers.

6. B   Mountain lions, which are second-order heterotrophs, decreased in population size. Deer, which are first-order heterotrophs, increased in population size.

7. B   Because plants release oxygen, decreasing their numbers would decrease the oxygen released.

8. D   The scenario, including the overgrowth of algae, is an example of eutrophication.

9.

Effect of ecosystem alteration	Process affected
Loss of trees	Decreased transpiration
Loss of lake	Decreased runoff
Decrease in percolation	Decreased groundwater
Decrease in evaporation	Decreased condensation

Lesson 2.3

Interactions Among Populations, p. 26

1.   1️⃣ Select . . . ▼

      B. water

      2️⃣ Select . . . ▼

      C. increase

2.   In this scenario, _____food_____ became a limiting factor. As the cougar population declined due to hunting, the deer population increased due to reduced predation. As the deer population increased, the availability of food diminished due to competition. Eventually the deer population declined because there was not enough food available to feed all of the deer.

3.   According to the following figures, the estimated carrying capacity for this stable moose population in the park is _____144.8_____.

4. A   The graph shows that the population fluctuates only slightly around the line of carrying capacity, meaning that it will remain relatively stable over time.

5. D   Because the insects are outside of the lake and do not interact with the fish, their population is least likely to affect the population of fish.

6. C   The graph shows that in the absence of population-limiting factors, the population would increase exponential, far exceeding the carrying capacity.

7. C   In a commensal relationship, one organism benefits from a second organism while the second organism neither benefits nor is harmed. The beetles benefit from the ants, but because the food is not missed, they do not harm the ants.

8. **A** In a parasitic relationship, one organism takes nutrients from the living body of another organism and, in doing so, may harm but does not immediately kill the other organism. Because the fungus damages and ultimately kills the tree, it is considered a parasite.

9. **A** In this scenario, hawks are predators of mice. Therefore, as the population of hawks increases, predation increases and the population of mice decreases.

10. **A** Prey are most likely to benefit from camouflage because they can use it to remain undetected by predators.

Lesson 2.4

Disruptions to Ecosystems, p. 29

1. **C** For a time, the volcanic event displaced animals when they fled to safety. When they returned to the area, they carried and dropped, in their dung, seeds of plants new to the recovering ecosystem of Mount St. Helens.

2. **D** One definition of *avalanche* is a sudden, overwhelming quantity of something. The eruption of Mount St. Helen was preceded by an earthquake. This caused the north face of the mountain to tumble down in a mass of rock and debris—an *avalanche*.

3. **D** When a river rises above its banks and flows over a floodplain, the floodwaters deposit a layer of nutrient-rich sediment. This adds much-needed nourishing substances to soil depleted by farming.

4. **D** Among threats to the bald eagle's survival was lead poisoning from eating waterfowl that had been shot with lead bullets by hunters. Therefore, in 1991, lead shot was phased out for hunting waterfowl.

5. DDT was a pesticide. It was banned because birds that were exposed to DDT began to lay eggs with fragile shells. Fragile eggshells may have been one cause of the bald eagle's shrinking population. DDT was banned in 1972, and according to the chart, the bald eagle population began to rise a year or so later. This is most likely because the DDT was no longer affecting the eggshells, so more of the young were hatching successfully.

6. **B** The release of carbon dioxide into the atmosphere from the burning of fossil fuels has contributed to a rise in global temperatures. This has led to increased melting of polar ice caps and an associated rise in sea levels. These are linked to loss of habitat along shorelines, due to rising water levels.

7. **B** No matter how well intended the effort, there can be unintended consequences linked to altering an ecosystem. Every organism in an ecosystem plays an important role. When organisms are removed or a new one is introduced, it is not always possible to accurately predict how others in the food chain will be affected.

8. **B** An ecosystem is a community of organisms that interact with each other and their environment. Whenever overhunting significantly reduces one species, other species in the food chain are affected. These changes influence a community's biodiversity and can disrupt the entire ecosystem.

9. Biodiversity is the variety of species in an area. Before wolves were reintroduced into the park, the elk population had grown sufficiently large to negatively impact the environment. The elk were damaging the cottonwood and aspen trees, which fed beaver and provided homes for birds. This disruption of the ecosystem reduced the populations of beaver and birds, and reduced the biodiversity within the park.

10. According to the passage, wolves ___increased___ the biodiversity of Yellowstone National Park.

11. **A** In an ecosystem, whenever one species is removed, other species in the food chain are affected. Removal of the wolves from Yellowstone National Park upset the natural balance and reduced the biodiversity of the ecosystem. While the elk seemed to thrive, other species of plants and animals declined. By reintroducing the wolves into the ecosystem, this imbalance may be corrected and equilibrium restored.

Lesson 3.1

Cells: Basic Units of Life, p. 32

1. **B** Both paragraphs address various ways in which the theory that microscopic life can arise on its own out of nonliving matter was disproven.

2. **A** The passage explains that spontaneous generation was disproved by the fact that once microbes such as bacteria are killed, they do not lead to new life forms. Therefore, spontaneous generation holds that living things can be created from nonliving things.

3. Once all of the bacteria on the instruments are killed, they do not reappear. This shows that living organisms cannot create themselves out of nonliving matter.

4.

Variable	Type
Time	Independent
Cheesecloth	Independent
Maggots	Dependent

5. **D** Redi's experiment shows that maggots cannot arise out of thin air, which is the basic tenet of the theory of spontaneous generation.

6. **C** Allowing the meat to be exposed to air, but not the flies, proved that maggots were created by flies. This showed that maggots do not spontaneously appear and are not created by microorganisms in the air.

7. **B** Nerve tissue is responsible for relaying sensory information.

8.

1. A

2. C

3. B

4. D

9. **D** Large cells require a large surface area in order to absorb enough materials to support cell metabolism. They require more materials than small cells because they have greater metabolic needs.

10. **C** Epithelial tissue is responsible for forming linings and coverings for body parts.

11. Blood is considered a type of ___connective___ tissue.

12. Cell specialization allows each cell to function more effectively because it is equipped to do a specific job.

13.

Tissue type	Function
Connective	A
Epithelial	B
Muscle	D
Nerve	C

Lesson 3.2

Cell Structure and Function, p. 35

1. **B** The cell membrane controls how substances pass into and out of a cell.

2. **A** Vacuoles are a place where cells can store resources and wastes. Therefore, cells in an orange would use vacuoles to store liquid.

3.

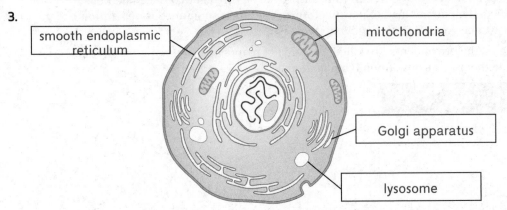

4. **D** The purpose of chloroplasts is to convert sunlight into energy in the form of glucose. Organisms that obtain energy in the form of glucose from other sources do not require chloroplasts.

5. Unlike prokaryotic cells, ___eukaryotic___ cells have a nucleus and organelles enclosed by membranes.

6. **B** The cell wall is a rigid outer layer that supports the cell and protects it from harm.

7. **B** The cell wall is the only cell part listed that plant and animal cells do not share.

8. **A** The passage states that bacterial cells do not contain a nucleus.

9. **D** Binary fission applies to genetic material that is not bound by a nucleus. Therefore, eukaryotic cells cannot engage in binary fission.

10. **D** In diffusion, substances move from areas of high concentration to low concentration until equilibrium is reached. Therefore, diffusion allows substances to spread evenly throughout the body.

11. In ___active___ transport, carrier proteins are needed to move materials across the cell membrane. Active transport involves the movement of materials from an area of low concentration to an area of high concentration. Because the materials are moving in the direction that is against their concentration gradient, carrier proteins must use energy and do the work of transporting them.

12. **D** The passage states that diffusion works by moving the substance from an area of high concentration to an area of lower concentration.

13. **C** Cells use active transport to reverse diffusion, and carrier proteins are essential to the function of active transport.

Lesson 3.3

Plant Structure and Function, p. 38

1. **A** Mosses are nonvascular plants, lacking vascular tissue to move water and other materials inside the plant. They must take water directly into their cells through osmosis, so they must grow close to a water source. Their life cycles are tied to damp places.

2. **C** Gymnosperms are vascular plants that produce seeds that are not enclosed within a fruit, but form seeds in cones. The leaves of most gymnosperms are scale-like or needle like.

3. **B** In science, a dependent variable is the variable that reacts to other variables, specifically the independent or manipulated variable, in an experiment. In this experiment, plant movement is influenced by, or dependent upon, the amount of light (manipulated variable) to which the plant is subjected.

4. Ferns, redwoods, and orchids are all examples of <u>vascular plants</u>.

5. Both gymnosperms and angiosperms are vascular plants. They both produce seeds. However, the seeds of a gymnosperm are not enclosed within a fruit, as they are with an angiosperm. Also, a gymnosperm does not produce flowers, while an angiosperm does.

6. **D** When conducting a study, well-focused questions will yield the best data. Maple tree fruit is designed to be dispersed by wind. Therefore, to study the dispersal range of the maple tree seeds, a key question to consider is how the winged traits of the fruit will interact with wind, affecting the dispersal.

7. Nonvascular plants take in water only through osmosis. They must stay in contact with moisture so that water can flow in or out of their cells as needed. Therefore, they are tied to damp places and grow close to the source of water.

8. **A** Nonvascular plants take in water from their surroundings through osmosis. Hot, dry conditions would increase the evaporation rate of water from the surrounding environment and thus lower the water concentration in the environment. Therefore, water molecules would move from a place of higher concentration of water inside the plant cells to a place of lower concentration of water in the environment.

9.
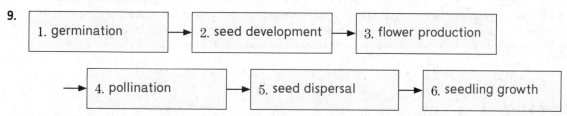

10. **C** An organic molecule is any compound of carbon and another element or a radical. A carbohydrate is a large organic molecule consisting of carbon (C), hydrogen (H), and oxygen (O) atoms.

11. **B** Unused energy in plants takes the form of carbohydrates, such as starch and sugar, and lipids. Taproots serve primarily as a storage organ for the food and energy sources produced by plants.

12. **D** In angiosperms, flowers are the main reproductive organs of a plant. Sepals are the green leaf-like structures surrounding the bud. Their function is to protect the delicate tissues inside.

13. **D** In angiosperms, flowers are the main reproductive organs of a plant. The stamen, the male reproductive organ, consists of an anther, which produces pollen grains. Pollen grains contain the sperm that will fertilize the plant eggs.

Lesson 3.4

Energy and Cells, p. 41

1. **B** According to the graph, the blue and orange ranges contain the highest spikes in the percent of light absorbed.

2. **D** A speculative statement cannot be substantiated by the evidence provided. Although chlorophyll that absorbs blue light is mentioned in the data, the concept of evolution is not.

3. **D** The graph shows that green light is not absorbed by the chlorophyll. Therefore, the plant most likely is green in color, and mushrooms are the only option that is not green in color.

4. **B** The passage states that during photosynthesis, plant cells use sunlight as an energy source to produce sugar, which is considered a form of chemical energy.

5. **C** A speculative statement cannot be substantiated by the evidence provided. Although respiration is mentioned in the passage, its potential to power medical devices is not.

6. **C** Cellular respiration breaks down glucose whereas photosynthesis creates glucose. Therefore, the reactions work in reverse of each other.

7.

Stages of Cellular Respiration
1. A
2. D
3. B
4. C

8. C Oxygen does not appear in the equation; therefore it is considered anaerobic (a term applied to chemical processes that do not require oxygen).

9. Oxygen does not appear in the fermentation equation. Therefore, cells that lack access to oxygen can utilize this process to release stored energy.

10. A Cellular respiration is a more efficient process than fermentation; therefore it produces more energy than fermentation.

11. A Whereas cheese and yogurt rely on lactic acid fermentation and alcohol relies on alcohol fermentation, butter relies on the process of churning cream, not fermenting it.

12. C In cellular respiration, two molecules of ATP provide the energy to break a glucose molecule down into two molecules of pyruvate and produces two molecules of ATP. However, during lactic acid fermentation, the pyruvate is changed into lactic acid instead of more ATP molecules.

Lesson 3.5

Mitosis and Meiosis, p. 44

1. Prokaryotes reproduce through binary fission while ____eukaryotes____ undergo a process known as the cell cycle. The DNA of eukaryotes is contained in a nucleus whereas in prokaryotes it is not bound to a nucleus.

2. A During the gap phases, cells must expand in size in order to accommodate the processes of replication and dividing in the other phases.

3. A The purpose of cell division is to create two identical cells. Therefore, in preparation the cell must create two sets of identical genetic information and create enough cellular material to create two cells.

4.

First
C
B
D
A
Last
E

5. B The purpose of the diagram is to show the process of cell replication, the most important feature of which is the duplication of genetic material, or chromosomes.

6. B During anaphase, the third stage, spindle fibers shorten and split the centromeres apart. As the fibers continue to shorten, sister chromatids move to opposite ends of the cell.

7. C Each sentence in the passage is focused on the various circumstances under which mutations can arise during cell replication.

8. C The passage states that after a chromosome is replicated, a mutated gene can be passed on. Therefore, it can be inferred that genes are part of a chromosome.

9. C During telophase II, spindle fibers break down. Chromosomes uncoil and nuclear envelopes form, creating two nuclei.

10. The two cells created in the diagram must undergo a second round of cell division, known as meiosis II, in order to create a total of four gametes. Each of these four gametes has only half the number of chromosomes as the two cells shown in telophase I in the diagram.

11. A During meiosis, or sexual reproduction, the nucleus divides twice to reduce the number of chromosomes by half. Sister chromatids must be split apart in Meiosis II in order to split the number of chromosomes in half.

12. The protein structures responsible for pulling apart the chromosomes during cell division are known as _____spindle_____ fibers.

13. All of the cells in the human body contain 46 chromosomes except for the _____gametes_____, which cannot carry the same number of chromosomes as those of other parts of the body.

14. B Gametes are reproductive cells produced by meiosis. Zygote begin the growth process which is the product of mitosis.

Lesson 4.1

Basic Principles of Genetics, p. 47

1. C 20 percent of the population has the dominant trait, so 80 percent has the recessive trait.

2. B The data show that dominant alleles are not the most common type of allele in the three populations shown so it is reasonable to conclude that dominant alleles are not always the most common type of allele in a population. There is not enough information, however, to make the conclusion that dominant alleles are almost never the most common type of allele.

3. Population _____C_____ has the greatest number of individuals with the dominant trait. In this population, there are _____40_____ individuals with the dominant trait.

4.

Traits Exhibited	Allele Combination
tall plant with white flowers, round seeds, and green pods	GgppTTWW
tall plant with purple flowers, round seeds, and green pods	GGPPTtWw
short plant with purple flowers, wrinkled seeds, and yellow pods	ggPpttww

5. A The table shows pea plant traits that have two forms, one dominant and one recessive. Most traits are not inherited through such simple patterns.

6. B All statements are false except the statement that sister chromatids are present only after replication. During replication, a strand of DNA makes an exact copy. The two exact copies are called sister chromatids.

7. Heredity occurs through chromosomes, which are passed from parent to offspring. A person has homologous pairs of chromosomes, one from each parent. Genes are found along the chromosomes. Genes determine traits. For example, Mendel's pea plants had genes for flower color and seed shape. Alleles are different forms of a gene. Mendel's pea plants had two alleles for each trait he studied. Flower color, for example, had an allele for white flower color and an allele for purple flower color.

8. 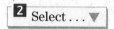 Select . . . ▼

D. chromosomes

2 Select . . . ▼

B. mitosis

9. D Gametes are necessary to the process of sexual reproduction, such as pollination and fertilization. The other processes listed do not involve the production of gametes.

10. C Meiosis reduces the number of chromosomes in a cell by one half. This allows the preservation of the appropriate chromosome count when two gametes unite in fertilization.

11. B This is the only combination that includes one allele from each of the allele pairs possessed by the parent—the gamete must have one and only one allele from each pair.

Lesson 4.2

Probability of Traits, p. 50

1. **B** In pea plants, green seed color is the recessive trait. In order to express the recessive trait, a pea plant that has a green phenotype must have two recessive alleles, as represented by the genotype *yy*.

2. **C** An organism with two different alleles for a trait is heterozygous for that trait. The genotype *Pp* denotes a trait expressed by one dominant allele and one recessive allele.

3. The phenotype of an organism describes its __physical traits__. Genotype describes the genetic makeup of an organism. Genotype determines the phenotype of an organism based upon what combination of dominant and recessive alleles the genotype contains. For example, tallness is a dominant trait in pea plants. The phenotype of a tall plant is described as tall, but its genotype may be made up of two alleles for tallness (*TT*) or one allele for tallness and one for shortness (*Tt*). By contrast, a pea plant whose phenotype is short, can have only one genotype (*tt*) because this plant must inherit two recessive alleles in order to display the shortness trait.

4. **D** A combination of alleles influences an organism's phenotype. In order to express a recessive trait, such as standard ears, an organism must have two recessive alleles. Based on the Punnett square predictions, each kitten has only a 25% change of inheriting two recessive alleles for standard ears. Each kitten has a 75% change of inheriting at least one dominant allele and, therefore, expressing the curled ear trait.

5.

	Y	y
y	Yy	yy
y	Yy	yy

6.

	R	R
R	RR	RR
r	Rr	Rr

7. In the cross shown, *R* represents round seeds and r represents wrinkled seeds. Based upon this information, the probability that an offspring from this cross will have wrinkled seeds is _____0%_____.

8. The Punnett square indicates that 100% of the offspring will have round seeds because each offspring inherits at least one dominant allele (*R*) for the trait. Of the offspring produced, 50% are expected to be homozygous for round seeds (*RR*) because each of these offspring will inherit a dominant allele from each parent. The remaining 50% will be heterozygous for round seeds because they will inherit only one dominant allele for the trait from the two parents.

9. **C** Blood groups in humans are determined by more than one pair of alleles.

10. **A** *X* and *Y* chromosomes are sex chromosomes that determine sex (male or female). Genetic males carry one *X* and one *Y* chromosome.

11. The probability is 12.5%.
    $2 \div 16 = 0.125$
    $1.25 \times 100 = 12.5\%$

12. B To be a carrier for colorblindness, a daughter needs to receive the allele combination X^CX^c. There is only a 25% change for an offspring resulting from this cross to have this genotype.

13. The designation _____X^C_____ and/or _____X^c_____ in the Punnett square indicates that color blindness is a sex-linked trait carried on the X chromosome.

14. D Like color blindness, hairy ears is a sex-linked trait. However, the recessive gene for hairy ears is carried on the *Y* chromosome. Genetic males carry one *X* and one *Y* chromosome. Genetic females carry two *X* chromosomes. Therefore, only male children are able to inherit the *Y*-linked trait for hairy ears, whereas in the illustration only males were affected.

Lesson 4.3

Common Ancestry, p. 53

1. A Trilobite fossils have been found in layers of sedimentary rock deep in the Grand Canyon, while coral fossils are found in layers along rim of the canyon. Lower layers of rock are older than upper layers. Therefore, a fossil in a lower layer must be older than a fossil in an upper layer.

2. A Darwin proposed that all forms of life change over time. He also proposed that, as the environment changes, organisms must adapt in order to survive. Organisms that are not able to adapt will die out.

3.

   1 Select . . . ▼   **3** Select . . . ▼

   A. species   C. offspring

   2 Select . . . ▼

   B. interbreed

4. B The theory of UCA proposes that every living organism may be linked back to a single common ancestor. The similarity in genetic material shared by seemingly unrelated organisms offers support of this theory of a shared common ancestor.

5. Adaptation is a change in a species that makes it better suited for its environment. As organisms adapt, they develop and pass on new traits to the next generation. In time, some members of a population may become isolated from the original population. Through adaptation, this new group will develop its own distinct traits, passing them on until the group is so changed that it no longer is able to reproduce with the original population. It is then considered a new species and has added to the biodiversity of life.

6. A The theory of UCA suggests that the ancestry of every organism that ever lived can be traced back to a single primitive ancestor. A cladogram shows evolutionary relationships and the points where species appear to have diverged from common ancestors.

7. B Cladograms demonstrate the evolutionary relationships among organisms. They are organized around structural traits shared by related organisms. The more structural traits that two organisms share, the closer their evolutionary relationship.

8.

Step 1	Step 2	Step 3	Step 4	Step 5	Step 6
Choose the species you would like to compare.	Choose structural traits to compare.	Make a table matching organisms and traits.	List or draw each organism.	Draw circles around the species that share a trait.	Use this information to construct a cladogram.

Lesson 4.4

Heredity: Genetic Variations and Expression, p. 56

1. **C** The illustration shows the process of crossing over. During this process, DNA from the father or DNA from the mother is exchanged along the chromosomes. As a result, each gamete receives a new combination of genes, which adds to the variety of traits within a population.

2. **C** Linked genes are genes that are found on the same chromosome. Because they are found on the same chromosome, linked genes are usually inherited together. If crossing over occurs between the positions of two linked genes, then the linked genes can be separated.

3. **A** Before a cell can reproduce, it must first replicate, or make a copy of, its DNA. Chemicals in the body induce cells at the site of a wound to begin the process of replication and reproduction to repair the injury.

4. **A** A mutation is a random, permanent change that occurs in the genetic material of a cell. Mutations can be caused by errors during normal processes related to genetic material and are often expressed in serious diseases, such as cancer or cystic fibrosis.

5.

Genetic Information Lost (switched or added at the chromosome level)	Error in DNA Coding within Egg or Sperm Cells	Errors During Replication that affect Body Cells
1. Down Syndrome 2. May be passed on, parent to child.	3. Cystic fibrosis 4. May be passed on, parent to child	5. Cancer 6. Cannot be passed on, parent to child.

6. 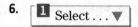 **1** Select . . . ▼

   A. crossing over

   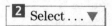 **2** Select . . . ▼

   D. matching chromosomes

7. **C** During the process of cell replication, an extra copy of DNA is made. When the bacteria cell containing human DNA reproduces, a copy of all the DNA in the cell is made. As the bacteria cells continue to reproduce, the DNA of each cell copy will contain human DNA.

8. As used in the passage above, the word trait means ___a quality or characteristic that is genetically determined___.

9. **A** During the process of cell replication, an extra copy of DNA is made. As the cells continue to divide, each new cell contains another copy of the DNA. When the bacterial cell containing human DNA reproduces, every cell produced also contains human DNA.

Lesson 4.5

Selection and Adaptation, p. 59

1. **C** Darwin's observations of variations in the shells and necks of the tortoises on the Galápagos caused him to question why and how these differences arose in the species.

2. **A** Darwin's observations of the different finch species enabled him to recognize that the beak shapes of the finches differed according to the types of food they ate.

3.

1.	D
2.	B
3.	C
4.	A

4. **C** Mimicry occurs when a harmless organism looks like a different, more dangerous organism. The ability of a nonpoisonous pine snake to vibrate and rattle its tail helps it to escape predators that mistake the snake for a poisonous rattlesnake.

5. **D** The birds with large beaks would starve because their beaks are not well suited for the small seeds. They have too much beak mass to easily manipulate small seeds.

6.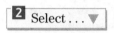

B. camouflage

A. mimicry

7. **A** Observations of the foots structure of the birds and the ways in which the birds move about in their environments reveal that the webbed feet of the duck is an adaptation that is suited to swimming and the long, wide toes of the heron are adapted to walking or wading through water.

8. Kangaroos and koalas are examples of adaptive radiation because both species evolved from a common ancestor, but have adapted different structures that help them survive in their environments. Both kangaroos and koalas are marsupials, a characteristic which indicates that they share a common ancestry. However, each animal is suited to a very different lifestyle. For example, a kangaroo is suited to life on the ground and is able to travel long distances to obtain food. By contrast, a koala is small and spends most of its time in the eucalyptus trees it uses as food.

9. **C** A species is defined as a group of potentially interbreeding individuals. When the environment has changed so much that new species arise, it is unlikely they will still be able to reproduce with each other. Each species' genetics will be different enough that they are not compatible with each other.

Lesson 5.1

Motion, p. 62

1. **C** There are three points on the graph where the speed is 7.8 m/s: 4 s, 22 s, and 31 s. Of these, only 22 s is given as an answer choice.

2. **B** Deceleration is indicated by a line with a negative slope, such as between 0 and 5 seconds, and again between 30 and 35 seconds.

3. **A** The car's initial speed is 6 m/s at 10 s, and its final speed at 30 s is 9 m/s. Acceleration $= \frac{(9 \text{ m/s} - 6 \text{ m/s})}{(30 \text{ s} - 10 \text{ s})} = \frac{(3 \text{ m/s})}{20 \text{ s}} = 0.15 \text{ m/s}^2$

4. **D** The difference between the plane's final and initial positions is 75 km, and the difference in the plane's final and initial times is 9.0 min. Convert the time to hours by dividing 9.0 min by 60 min/h, and recall that velocity consists of speed and direction.

velocity $= \frac{(75 \text{ km, east})}{(9 \text{ min/60 min/h})} = \frac{(75 \text{ km, east})}{(0.15 \text{ h})} = 500 \text{ km/h, east}$

5. If the cart has no acceleration, it has constant velocity. As velocity has both speed and direction information, and velocity is constant, then both speed and direction are unchanging. Because an object at rest has a constant speed of 0, the cart at rest is a special case of zero acceleration.

6. **C** Because force is the slope of the line, it follows that the smaller the force required to change the momentum of an object, the greater the interval of time that is required to make that change. Another way of putting this is that the line with the smallest slope (force) is the line that extends over the longest interval of time.

7. **B** Find the position on the horizontal axis that corresponds to 7.50 s (halfway between 5.00 and 10.0 s), and note which point on each line corresponds to 4700 kg · m/s (slightly below the 5.00×10^3 kg · m/s mark). This point is designated B.

8. **C** You need to use the information provided to calculate momentum:
momentum = mv = (52.0 kg)(4.5 m/s, south) = 234 kg · m/s, south

9. **C** From the law of conservation of momentum, initial momentum of the system = final momentum of the system, or

$$m_{water}v_{water,initial} + m_{student/bucket/board}v_{student/bucket/board,initial} =$$
$$m_{water}v_{water,final} + m_{student/bucket/board}v_{student/bucket/board,final}.$$

Because everything is initially at rest, this equation simplifies to
$$-m_{water}v_{water,final} = m_{student/bucket/board}v_{student/bucket/board,final}.$$

Inserting the values, and noting that the mass of water must be subtracted from the total system mass, $-(10.0$ kg$)(2.50$ m/s, south$) = (80.0$ kg $- 10.0$ kg$)v_{student/bucket/board,final}.$

Rearranging the equation:
$$v_{student/bucket/board,final} = \frac{(-25.0 \text{ kg} \cdot \text{m/s, south})}{(70.0 \text{ kg})} = -0.357 \text{ m/s, south, or}$$
$$v_{student/bucket/board,final} = 0.357 \text{ m/s, north.}$$

10. Suppose the mass of the balloon equals 0.010 kg, and the balloon moves to the right with a uniform speed of 0.10 m/s. The total momentum (momentum = mass × velocity) of the balloon-air system is ___0 kg · m/s___. The law of conservation of momentum states that if no other forces act on the objects, their total momentum remains the same after they interact. Because the balloon and air are initially at rest (a constant speed of 0 kg · m/s), the combined momentum of the released air and the moving balloon equals 0 kg · m/s.

11. **B** When the system is initially at rest, the balloon moves to the right with the same momentum as the air moves toward the left. If the balloon already has motion to the right, the extra momentum will cause it to continue even faster in that direction.

Lesson 5.2

Forces and Newton's Laws of Motion, p. 65

1. The man exerts a force of 40 N on the table (F_A), while the woman exerts a force of 60 N (F_B). The net force (F_{net}) acting on the table is ___100 N___.

2. **C** You need to calculate acceleration using the information given:
$a = \frac{F_{net}}{d}$; $a = 60$ N $+ 60$ N $\div 10$ m; $a = 120$ n · m/s$^2 \div 10$ m; $a = 12$ m/s^2

3. **D** The more mass an object has, the greater its inertia.

4. The water exerts a reaction force of equal magnitude in the opposite direction on the boat which causes it to begin moving. To remain in one place, the action and reaction forces need to balance each other by acting on the same object with the same magnitude of force in opposing directions. Here, the action and reaction forces have the same magnitude per Newton's third law of motion, but the forces are not acting on the same object because the action force is transmitted by the oars to the water, but the reaction force acts on the boat. As a result, the boat is pushed through the water.

5. **C** You need to calculate average acceleration using the information given:

$\frac{a = F_{net}}{m}$; $a = 15$ N $+ 30$ N $\div 30$ kg; $a = 45$ N $\cdot$ m/s$^2 \div 30$ kg; $a = 1.5$ m/s^2

6. Gravity and magnetism are examples of action-at-a-distance forces. Such forces are able to exert a push or a pull on another object without being in direct contact with the object. By contrast, friction is a contact force that acts only on objects that are physically touching or in contact with each other.

7. The force is less than 30 N to the right. The rope will move in the direction of the larger force, so the pulling force of 30N to the left must be greater than the pulling force to the right.

8. **D** Motion results when unbalanced forces act on an object. Thus when the forces acting on an object are balanced and the net force is 0, no movement occurs.

9. The diagram shows five pairs of balls. The gravitational force is weakest between the balls shown in pair number _____1_____ and strongest between the balls shown in pair number _____4_____.

10. 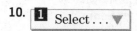 Select . . . ▼

    D. decrease by one-fourth

    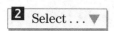 Select . . . ▼

    A. double

11. **C** You need to calculate weight using the information given:
    $W = mg$; $W = 50$ kg $\times 9.8$ m/s^2; $W = 490$ kg $\cdot$ m/s^2; $W = 490$ N

12. **D** You need to calculate mass of the individual on Earth and acceleration due to gravity on Jupiter using the information given:

    To find mass on Earth:
    $W = mg$ or $\frac{W}{g} = m$; Earth weight is $\frac{539 \text{ N}}{9.8 \text{ m/s}^2} = m$; 539 kg $\cdot$ m/s$^2 \div 9.8$ m/s$^2 = m$; $m = 55$ kg.

    To find acceleration due to gravity on Jupiter:
    $\frac{W_{Jupiter}}{m} = g$; $1{,}273.8$ kg $\cdot$ m/s$^2 \div 55$ kg $= 23.16$ m/s^2

Lesson 5.3

Work and Simple Machines, p. 68

1. **A** Work is measured in newton-meters, or joules (J). The newton (N) is a unit of force. The watt (W) is a unit of power. Meter per second squared (m/s^2) is a unit of acceleration.

2. **D** First find force. $F = 10$ kg $\times 4$ m/s$^2 = 40$ N. Then use the force to find work.
   $W = 40$ N $\times 30$ m $= 1200$ J.

3.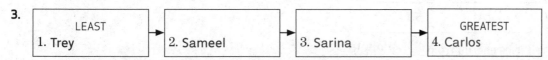

4. **B** An inclined plane is a simple machine that requires the user to exert a smaller force over a longer distance. Wedges and screws are both types of inclined planes.

5. Although the distance and force change, the work is the same in each case—10 J. So they need to revise their hypothesis to indicate that the ramp decreases the force they need to exert to do the work, but does not change the amount of work they need to do. A new hypothesis might be: If the length of the ramp increases, then the force required to move the box decreases.

6. 1) All three levers are simple machines are levers that consist of a rigid part that rotates about a fulcrum. 2) They all make work easier in some way.

7.

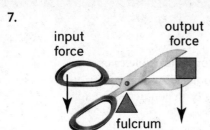 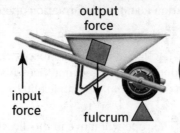 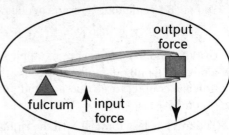

8. A Substitute the given information into the equation for mechanical advantage: $MA = \frac{720 \text{ N}}{60 \text{N}} = 12$.

9. C Mechanical advantage is equal to the output force divided by the input force. If distance is multiplied, then force is decreased. As a result, the output force is less than the input force so the mechanical advantage is less than 1.

10. B The force required is least for Setup A and greatest for Setup C. This means that the mechanical advantage is also greatest for Setup A and least for Setup C. In terms of lengths, the diagram shows that length x is least and y greatest for Setup A. Therefore, the ratio of y to x is greatest for Setup A. As this ratio increases, the mechanical advantage must increase.

11. A Substitute the given information into the equation for mechanical advantage: $MA = \frac{1800 \text{ N}}{900 \text{ N}} = 2$.

12. If the mechanic alters the design of the pulley system, the mechanical advantage becomes 6. The force that will be required to lift the engine will be ____300 N____.

Lesson 6.1

Types of Energy and Energy Transformations, p. 71

1. D The skateboard has a gravitational force acting on it, and which will do work on the skateboard in pulling it downward to the bottom of the incline. Therefore its initial potential energy is gravitational.

2. A You need to calculate gravitational potential energy given the information provided:
$GPE = mgh = (6.50 \text{ kg})(9.81 \text{ m/s}^2)(3.20 \text{ m}) = 204 \text{ J}$

3.

KE (J)	Mass (kg)	Speed (m/s)
6.00	0.750	4.00
4.69	1.50	2.50
12.00	1.50	4.00
2.34	0.750	2.50
0.844	0.750	1.50

4. A photovoltaic cell uses energy from ____sunlight____.

5. B The photocell converts incoming radiant energy (such as sunlight) to electrical energy.

6. A The magnetic field that Ørsted observed was present around a wire carrying electric current. Therefore, the current (moving electrons) are believed to cause the magnetic field.

7. D The electrical current from the wire would create a magnetic field, which would cause the magnetic compass needle to move.

8. B At $d = 0$, the block is at the highest point on the incline plane, so all of its energy is gravitational potential energy.

9. D Kinetic and potential energy change as the speed and position of the block change. As potential energy decreases, kinetic energy increases. However, the total mechanical energy (the sum of potential and kinetic energies) is a constant.

10. The sloping line would indicate a decrease in total mechanical energy (that is, kinetic plus gravitational potential energy). Because energy is conserved, this means that the "lost" energy takes a different form, which in this system would be a gain in heat, caused by an increase in the kinetic energy of the particles making up the block and plane. This increase would be caused by friction between the block and the plane.

Lesson 6.2

Sources of Energy, p. 74

1. **B** Atoms split apart and lose subatomic particles, or decay, when hit by high-speed neutrons in a nuclear reactor.

2.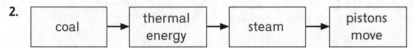

3. **A** The use of nuclear energy does not pollute the air since there is no combustion of fossil fuels.

4. The word **finite** as used in the statement means _nonrenewable_ or _limited_.

5. Based on the statement, you can infer that the use of natural energy sources causes _pollution or air pollution_.

6. **A** Biomass is organic matter. When either burned directly or processed into another type of fuel it is burned and then causes pollution.

7. **A** Since the population of the planet is growing and there are people with not enough to eat some people are concerned that using land that is currently growing food crops to grow crops for energy could cause food shortages.

8. **C** Since biomass can be converted into fuels it then can be easily transported.

9. I would not support the measure. I think it would be good if people could do so, but making it so people had to use a renewable energy source for heating and cooling would be unfair. It could be too expensive for some people. Also it may be difficult in some areas to obtain a source of renewable energy.

10. **B** If you were to draw a line in the direction that both petroleum and natural gas are going, the lines would cross around the mark for 2020.

11. **C** Nuclear is about at 8 quadrillion btu and natural gas is about 26 quadrillion btu. Petroleum is close to 34 quadrillion btu which is the same as nuclear and natural gas added together.

12. **A** These are political situations and the technology requires spending. Since there is a limited amount of money and other areas that need money it involves money and some of that is taxpayer money.

13. Technology can have causes that have political considerations. Fracking is a process that is controversial because of possible harm to the environment. It is a political question because people must make decisions after judging both the plus and minuses of a development.

Lesson 6.3

Heat, p. 77

1. **A** The greater the average kinetic energy of particles in a substance, the greater the temperature of the substance. Heat flows from substances at higher temperature to the substances at lower temperature. Therefore, heat involves the transfer of the kinetic energy between particles in substances at different temperatures.

2. **B** The iron atoms have greater average kinetic energies than do the water molecules, so the energy is transferred by heat from the iron to the water. This continues until both substances are at the same temperature.

3.

Energy	4.3×10^{-21} J	2.4×10^{-20} J	1.9×10^{-21} J	3.2×10^{-21} J	1.2×10^{-20} J
Temperature	205 K	1140 K	90 K	155 K	575 K

4. **C** In the radiator, heat conducts energy from the parts of the radiator that are at higher temperatures (the fluid inside the radiator), to the outer surface, which is closer to the temperature of the surrounding air.

5. **C** In convection, a fluid that is heated expands and becomes less dense. This causes it to move upward from the heat source and displace the fluid that is there. This cooler fluid moves downward, where it is heated, expands, and rises upward.

6. **A** Thermal conduction in a crystal requires particles that can move easily through the material, and so transfer kinetic energy from one part to another. The electrons in substance A can do this, so substance A is a better conductor of heat than substance B.

7. **C** As the car moves along the road, friction between the road and tires causes the rubber of the tires to heat. This heat is transferred to the air inside the tires, which causes it to expand. If the tires are overinflated when the air is cool, the expanded heated air may cause the tire to rupture in a "blowout."

8. **A** If the drill bit becomes too hot, it can be damaged. Friction between the rotating drill bit and the material being drilled increases the temperature of both as mechanical energy is converted to thermal energy. By spraying water, which has a large specific heat capacity, onto the bit, the bit's temperature can be kept low and damage prevented.

Lesson 6.4

Waves, p. 80

1. **C** All waves, whether they require a medium (mechanical waves) or not (electromagnetic waves), involve vibrations.

2. **B** The disturbance in a medium indicates that energy is present, yet there is no loss of energy in an ideal wave. The amount of energy that causes the disturbance is transferred entirely to the end of the wave.

3. The energy from the explosion is carried through air by waves. These waves are heard as a boom through sound waves in the air, but also transfer energy to the windows, shaking them. This energy is transferred back as a sound wave in the air, and is heard as the rattle of the glass.

4. The disturbance is evidence that suggests the presence of mechanical energy, which has caused the disturbance. The motion of uniform, repeated disturbances in the form of rising and falling water is evidence that indicates the presence of waves, which are transferring the energy from the point of disturbance to another location. The motion of the buoy, which rises and falls but does not move forward with the disturbances, indicates that matter is not transferred with the energy. Given this evidence, I can conclude that the disturbance is a wave.

5. **C** $v = f \times \lambda = 25 \text{ Hz} \times 0.030 \text{ m} = 0.75 \text{ m/s}$

6.

   A. crest

   B. trough

   A. transverse

   C. amplitude

7. **D** The light from a lightning flash travels at 300,000,000 meters per second, so it is seen almost at the same instant that it occurs. The sound of thunder caused by the heating and rapid contraction of the air during the flash travels about 1,100 meters per second, and so always arrives later. The farther away the lightning is, the longer it takes to hear the thunder.

8. **A** If the speed of light were so much slower that it would take several seconds to see the flash, then this time of travel would have to be taken into account along with the speed of sound waves in air in order to determine the distance to the lightning.

9.

LOWEST ENERGY			HIGHEST ENERGY
95 m	8.5×10^1 m	7.5×10^2 m	3.0×10^3 m

Lesson 7.1

The Structure of Matter, p. 83

1. **D**   Answer D requires the scientist to look further into the atom.

2. **B**   Because each product is made up of only one kind of atom, the products are elements.

3.   Overall, the helium atom is electrically neutral because the positive charges of the two protons in the nucleus are cancelled by the negative charges of the two electrons that orbit the nucleus. Neutrons are electrically neutral, so the presence of the neutrons does not impact the overall electrical charge of the atom.

4. **B**   Because chlorine is located to the right of the zigzag section of the periodic table, it is a nonmetal.

5. **A**   The periodic table indicates that chlorine has 17 protons because its atomic number is 17, so to be neutral, an atom of chlorine must also have 17 electrons.

6.   The number of neutrons in the nucleus of an atom of an element can be determined by subtracting the atomic number of the element provided by the periodic table from its atomic mass or mass number.

7. **A**   Because metals are generally good conductors of electricity, using the sample in place of a piece of wire in a working electrical circuit can be used to identify whether the sample is a metal. If the circuit works with the sample in place, the sample is most likely a metal. If the sample does not work, it is most likely not a metal.

8. **B**   Because the ratio of carbon (C) to hydrogen (H) in methane gas is 1 to 4, the formula for methane is CH_4.

9. $CaCO_3$

10.   Because it had the greatest increase in mass, sample 3 had the highest iron content.

Lesson 7.2

Physical and Chemical Properties of Matter, p. 86

1. **D**   A chemical property is one that can be observed only through changing the composition of matter. An antacid undergoes a chemical change as it reacts with water.

2. **C**   The density of a substance is the best property to use to distinguish it from others. Many substances can share the other properties listed.

3.

Stayed the Same	Changed
Color	Volume
Temperature	Mass
Density	Shape

4.   The sample begins in the _____liquid_____ state and changes to the _____gas_____ state.

5.   This type of change occurs when the sample absorbs thermal energy, thereby causing the particles of matter to move faster and to be farther apart.

6.   According to the graph, the melting point for the substance is _____60_____ degrees and the boiling point is _____120_____ degrees.

7.   The statement is not supported by the graph. In sections A, C, and E of the graph, the temperature does increase as thermal energy is absorbed. However, in sections B and D, thermal energy is absorbed, but the temperature does not change. Instead, the energy either separates the particles of matter out of the crystal lattice or spreads them farther apart.

8. **D** The horizontal line labeled as section D indicates a change of state. If energy is being absorbed from left to right across the graph, a liquid is changing to a gas through vaporization. If energy is being released from right to left across the graph, a gas is changing to a liquid through condensation.

9. **D** Elements are most likely to have similar physical and chemical properties if they are in the same group of the periodic table. A group is a vertical column of the table. Magnesium and calcium are the only two elements listed that are in the same group.

10. **B** An element acts like a metal when it conducts electricity and a nonmetal when it does not. An element that can have some properties of a metal and some properties of a nonmetal is a metalloid. Silicon is the only metalloid listed.

11. The statement is incorrect. The stability of elements increases from left to right across the periodic table. The elements in Group 1 at the left side of the table have one outermost electron. They are likely to give up their electron to become stable so they are highly reactive. The elements in Group 18 at the right side of the table have eight outermost electrons. They do not need to share electrons to have a complete set so they are very unreactive. So the elements along the left side of the table are highly reactive, but the elements along the right side of the table are not.

12. **C** Generally, elements in the same group have similar properties. Exceptions to this rule occur in the region of the periodic table where elements fall into different categories. In this case, carbon is in the nonmetal region of the table whereas lead is in the metal region.

Lesson 7.3

Chemical Reactions, p. 89

1. **D** The mass before and after the reaction differed because some matter escaped as gases. By stretching a balloon over the opening of the bottle, those gases can be captured. If the student then compares the masses of all the materials before and after, they should be the same.

2. **A** A chemical reaction involves a change in the composition of matter. When iron rusts, it reacts with air to form a new substance known as an iron oxide. The other changes involve only the appearance of matter.

3. **B** The paragraph relates to all of the topics, but its focus is to compare coefficients and subscripts.

4. In the chemical equation for photosynthesis shown below, _____6_____ molecules of water enter into the reaction.

5. **C** In the product, there are 2 molecules of aluminum oxide as shown by the coefficient. Each molecule contains 3 atoms of oxygen, as shown by the subscript. Therefore, $2 \times 3 = 6$.

6. $2CH_4 + 4O_2 \rightarrow 2CO_2 + 4H_2O$

7. $2H_2O_2 \rightarrow 2H_2O + O_2$

8. **D** The process represented would have to release energy. The only process listed that releases energy instead of absorbing it is cellular respiration, which is described as the process in which an animal uses glucose and oxygen.

9. Based on the change of energy shown, the graph represents an ___exothermic___ chemical reaction. The energy of the reactants is greater than the energy of the products. Therefore, energy was released during the reaction. A chemical reaction that releases energy is exothermic.

10. **B** The graph represents the reaction rate. It increases up to some peak, and then decreases. That peak is determined by temperature.

11. If the student raises the temperature to 30°C, the student will conclude that the rate increases continuously with temperature. The error is not raising the temperature enough to observe a limit in the rate of reaction. The student can correct the error by raising the temperature to at least 50°C before concluding the investigation.

Lesson 7.4

Solutions, p. 92

1.

Solute	Solvent	Solution
carbon dioxide	water	club soda
Zinc	copper	brass
Soap	water	detergent
oxygen	nitrogen	air

2. B   Oxygen dissolved in water is an example of a gas dissolved in a liquid.

3. C   As the temperature of the solvent increases, adding measured amounts of solute until saturation occurs will give accurate data of temperature and solubility.

4.   In the graph, _____temperature_____ is the independent variable, and _____solubility_____ is the dependent variable.

5. C   Using the curve for potassium bromide (the purple line) and reading upward from 90°C, the amount of solute is found to lie about halfway between 80 g and 120 g, or nearly 100 g.

6.   Under normal conditions, the pH of blood is slightly _____higher_____ than that of water. This makes blood _____more_____ basic than water. Even in a severe case of _____acidosis_____, when the pH of blood is 7.15, water is, by comparison, a(n) _____acid_____.

7. C   Hydrochloric acid is specifically mentioned as a strong acid, and by definition strong acids are those that dissociate completely.

8. A   Alkalosis occurs when blood pH is greater than 7.45, as in the case of a pH of 7.55.

9. B   For a given concentration of hydronium ions ($[H+]$), the pH may be found by taking the whole logarithm of $[H+]$ and multiplying the result by −1.

Therefore, pH depends on $[H+]$, or put differently, $[H+]$ is the independent variable, and pH is the dependent variable.

Lesson 8.1

The Atmosphere, p. 95

1. B   Sustaining life depends on the elements oxygen and nitrogen. Without those elements, neither animals nor plants could exist.

2. C   Choices A, B, and C would have a negative effect on promoting energy conservation. Choice C, reducing dependence on fossil fuels, is correct because there is a positive correlation between fossil fuel use and global warming.

3. A   The graph indicates that CO_2 levels showed a steady increase from 1880 through 2000.

4. B   The passage indicates that ultraviolet rays are the most damaging to living organisms, so the absorption of 97–99 percent of UV rays would be a major function of the ozone layer.

5. D   The passage states that living organisms are harmed by too much UV radiation, so ultraviolet radiation is energy harmful to humans.

6. D   The troposphere does not receive much UV radiation as the radiation is filtered out before reaching the troposphere, so it would not be possible for a layer such as the ionosphere to exist in the troposphere.

7. C   Students must read the diagram and compute rates of absorption and reflection. Half of the sun's energy is directly or indirectly absorbed by Earth's surfaces.

8.   Earth's atmosphere and surface absorb _____50_____ percent of the Sun's energy.

9. D The pattern that shows increased temperature levels over a prolonged period of time is called global warming.

10. Answers may vary but should include sound scientific principles. Responses may include reduced solar energy reaching Earth resulting in death of plant and animal life, destruction of crops, inability to replace food supplies, drastic changes in weather patterns, and/or an increasingly colder climate in formerly temperate or tropical zones.

Lesson 8.2

The Oceans, p. 98

1. A The diagram illustrates that precipitation falls as various forms of water.

2. C The diagram shows the movement of water from evaporation to condensation to precipitation and collection, all of which are movements of Earth's water.

3. C An estuary is a region where fresh river water meets salty ocean water, creating a less salty brackish water. The meltwater of a glacier also adds fresh water to salty ocean water, reducing the salinity of seawater.

4. In this scenario, the salinity of the water is the ___dependent___ variable and the location along the coast is the ___independent___ variable.

5. B Gravity is a force of attraction. The side of Earth closest to the Moon is affected by the Moon's gravitational field, which pulls or attracts the ocean water, causing changes in tides.

6. D Temperature depends on depth, with colder water in the depths of the ocean. Density also depends on depth, with less density at the ocean's surface.

7. A Plants depend on sunlight to produce food. Thus, plants will only survive in the ocean where they have adequate sunlight for photosynthesis.

8. In shallow areas of the ocean, sunlight may be transmitted through to the sea floor. Animal and plant life that depend on sunlight can exist at all depths of a shallow area of the sea. In the deep ocean, no light penetrates through to the ocean floor. The animals that exist at that depth will differ from the species that live in the shallow areas. In the deep ocean, plant life will exist only in areas reached by sunlight.

9.

Human Influences	Natural Influences
Overfishing	glacial meltwater
water pollution	surface evaporation
global warming	coral bleaching
	ebb tides

Lesson 8.3

Earth's Structure, Composition, and Landforms, p. 101

1. B The measurements shown on the diagram indicate that the mantle is the thickest layer of Earth.

2. A The thickness of the crust varies due to the presence of mountain ranges, valleys, trenches, and other major land features.

3. C Earth most closely resembles a golf ball because it has a hard center (the core), a thick middle section (the mantle), and a thin, uneven surface (the crust).

4. D Because Earth's crust is brittle and easily cracked, it is most like the plaster surface.

5. B The mantle discussed in this test is geological, a layer of Earth between the core and the crust.

6. Hematite is a mineral with a specific chemical makeup and a specific crystalline structure. She should test for iron content in each sample because hematite is an iron-based mineral. She should also compare the crystalline structures of the samples she has with the sample she knows to be hematite. All hematite has the same crystalline structure.

7.

Examples of Deposition	Examples of Weathering
soil laid down at the mouth of a river rocks and soil at the base of a landslide rubble left after a glacier recedes	underground water dissolving limestone ice cracking the surface of a rock a natural bridge carved by wind

8. According to the map, the Mid-Atlantic Ridge lies between the <u>North American</u> plate and the <u>Eurasian</u> plate.

9. D The two plates lie either side of the Mid-Atlantic Ridge, which passes directly under Iceland; thus, Iceland straddles both plates and the ridge itself.

10. D Convergent boundaries lie at the edges of two tectonic plates. Their movement causes them to collide, which usually results in the production of mountains, such as the Indian Plate and the Eurasian Plate producing the Himalaya Mountains.

Lesson 8.4

Earth Resources, p. 104

1.

Renewable Natural Resources	Nonrenewable Natural Resources
flowers, oxygen, river water, sunlight, wind	coal, diamonds, gold, oil, silver

2. C Only the Environmental Protection Agency does research into clean water, clean air, and reduced pollution.

3. D The use of fossil fuels in a major environmental and economic issue. There is only a limited supply of fossil fuels, and when that runs out, humans will need alternative fuel sources.

4. C The graph shows flat data concerning the use of oil to produce electricity.

5. A A coal-burning power plant produces high levels of air pollution. There is always a danger of pollutants affecting living organisms around such a plant. Nuclear plants do not emit pollutants, but when an accident occurs, radiation leaks threatened all living things.

6. Burning fossil fuels produces ash, smoke, and gases that pollute the atmosphere. Burning fossil fuels releases carbon dioxide into the atmosphere, which results in global warming.

7. C You must differentiate between economic value and environmental value. Ethanol's environmental value is that is reduces pollution and is based on renewable resources.

8. D You can draw the conclusion that Texas and California have invested heavily in wind power technology because they are the two largest producers of wind-power energy generation, topping the nearest competition dramatically.

9. A Midwest states generate more wind-powered energy than states in the East, many of which do not take advantage of this energy alternative.

Lesson 8.5

Interactions Between Earth's Systems, p. 107

1.

Type of Weather Data	Weather Occurrence
high humidity	Tropical rain storms
Temperature	A heat wave
high barometric pressure	Clear, pleasant weather
heavy winds	Broken tree branches and falling limbs

2. **A** Erosion is the act of moving particles from one place to another. Weathering is the break-down of rock into particles. The ripple pattern comes from erosion, and only wind will create the pattern.

3. **C** Planting trees reduces erosion by building a windbreak to hold the soil.

4. **C** Two forces act on the beach cliff. The first is physical weathering in which the wind and water break down the cliff face. The second is water erosion that carries the particles away from the cliff.

5. **B** The result of weathering and erosion on the beach cliff is that the face of the cliff recedes, while the area that is beach increases.

6. Answers will vary, but should include moderate wind, rain, and flood damage in the Bahamas, and extreme wind, rain, and flood damage in the United States. The wind speeds between the first and second sites increases by about 40 mph. The storm surge increases by 5–10 feet, which means the area damaged by flood will be larger in the U.S.

7. **A** According to the chart, 85 mph winds are typical of a Category 1 hurricane.

8. **B** A thunderstorm is the energy source that lifts a tornado from swirling air at ground level to a vertical funnel.

9. **D** Hurricanes needs a large supply of warm water to "feed" the storm system, which is why hurricanes begin over tropical waters.

Lesson 9.1

Structures in the Universe, p. 110

1. **D** The Big Bang theory states that over time, the universe's temperature has declined as the universe has expanded.

2. **C** Based on the timeline, galaxies formed about 3 billion years ago.

3.

1. Nebula	2. Protostar	3. Red giant	4. fusion	5. White dwarf

4. **C** When a supernova occurs, among the end products are heavy, metallic elements.

5. Every star in every galaxy in the universe is a source of energy. Within each star, including the Sun, nuclear energy heats the star and keeps it from collapsing due to the force of gravity. Meanwhile, each star's own energy and the _gravitational force_ between the star and other stars work together to keep the star within a path inside its own galaxy.

6. **C** As part of the process of building a new star, a protostar collects material and forms a denser, hot, glowing center.

7. **D** This is a comparison between a black hole that sucks material inward and downward and a common everyday occurrence. Of the items listed, the only one that sucks material both inward and downward is a whirlpool.

8.

9. Answers will vary, but the primary factor determining failure would be the scope of the project. First, our technology is far too limited for such a venture. The rockets would not be able to gather sufficient data to fully map each star or solar system, the cost would be enormous, and the project would take much longer than a hundred human life spans to complete.

10. **B** All matter has mass. All mass has gravity. While the gravitational force differs from body to body, all bodies in the universe have some level of gravity.

Lesson 9.2

Structures in the Solar System, p. 113

1.

Slowest 1. Venus	2. Earth	3. Neptune	Fastest 4. Jupiter

2. Neptune is about _____ six _____ times farther away from the Sun than Jupiter is.

3. An asteroid is a solid object smaller than a planet that orbits the Sun.

4. **B** The passage states that all the asteroids together would be less massive than Earth's Moon. Earth's Moon is not massive enough to be an independent planet so it is unlikely that the asteroids once formed an independent planet.

5. **C** Earth spins, or rotates, on its axis. One complete rotation takes 24 hours, or one day. If Earth were to spin more slowly, one day would take more than 24 hours so a day on Earth would last longer.

6. **B** Earth is tilted on its axis. As Earth revolves around the Sun, one hemisphere sometimes tilts toward the Sun whereas the other tilts away from the Sun. Locations in the hemisphere tilting away from the Sun experience winter.

7. **D** The information provided states that the gravitational force on the Moon is one-sixth that of Earth's force. By dividing the astronaut's weight by one-sixth, the astronaut's weight on the Moon can be determined. Knowing the astronaut's mass would be useful if the information states that the mass will not change.

8. **B** According to the graph, 5.2 billion years represents 4 half-lives. After 1 half-life, 50% remains. After 2 half-lives, half of that, or 25%, remains. After 3 half-lives, half of that, or 12.5%, remains. And after 4 half-lives, half of that, or 6.25%, remains.

9. According to the graph, the half-life of potassium-40 is _1.3 billion years_. To find the amount remaining, divide the amount by half for each half-life. According to the graph, 2.6 billion years is two half-lives. So after the first half-life, there will be 100 g ÷ 2, or 50 g remaining. After the second half-life, there will be 50 g ÷ 2, or 25 g remaining.

10. **C** According to the Law of Superposition, sedimentary rock forms in layers. If the layers are undisturbed, the age of the layers increases from top to bottom. Therefore, Layer C is younger and formed later than Layer E.

11. **B** Relative dating can be used to identify the order in which organisms lived, but not their actual ages or other specific details about the organisms.

| Order of Operations | The TI-30XS MultiView™ automatically evaluates numerical expressions using the Order of Operations based on how the expression is entered. | The correct answer is 23. |

Example
12 ÷ 2 × 3 + 5 =

Note that the 2 is **not** multiplied to the 3 before division occurs.

| Decimals | To calculate with decimals, enter the whole number, then ⬚, then the fractional part. | The correct answer is 17.016. |

Example
11.526 + 5.89 − 0.4 =

The decimal point helps line up the place value.

| Fractions | To calculate with fractions, use the ⬚ button. The answer will automatically be in its simplest form. | The correct answer is $\frac{15}{28}$. |

Example
$\frac{3}{7} \div \frac{4}{5} =$

This key combination works if the calculator is in Classic mode or MathPrint™ mode.

| Mixed Numbers | To calculate with mixed numbers, use the [2nd] [n/d] button. To see the fraction as an improper fraction, don't press the [2nd] [x10ⁿ] buttons in sequence below. | The correct answer is $39\frac{13}{15}$. |

Example
$8\frac{2}{3} \times 4\frac{3}{5} =$

This key combination only works if the calculator is in MathPrint™ mode.

| Percentages | To calculate with percentages, enter the percent number, then [2nd] [( ]. | The correct answer is 360. |

Example
72% × 500 =

Powers & Roots

To calculate with powers and roots, use the x^2 and ^ buttons for powers and the 2nd x^2 and 2nd ^ buttons for roots.

Example
$21^2 =$

[2] [1] [x^2] (enter)

The correct answer is 441.

Example
$2^8 =$

[2] [^] [8] (enter)

The correct answer is 256.

Example
$\sqrt{729} =$

(2nd) [x^2] [7] [2] [9] (enter)

The correct answer is 27.

Example
$\sqrt[5]{16807} =$

[5] (2nd) [^] [1] [6] [8] [0] [7] (enter)

The correct answer is 7.

You can use the (2nd) [x^2] and (2nd) [^] buttons to also compute squares and square roots.

Scientific Notation

To calculate in scientific notation, use the ($x10^n$) button as well as make sure your calculator is in Scientific notation in the (mode) menu.

The correct answer is 1.2011×10^5.

Example
$6.81 \times 10^4 + 5.201 \times 10^4 =$

[6] [.] [8] [1] ($x10^n$) [4] (sto ▶) [+]

[5] [.] [2] [0] [1] ($x10^n$) [4] (sto ▶) (enter)

When you are done using scientific notation, make sure to change back to Normal in the (mode) menu.

Toggle

In MathPrint™ mode, you can use the toggle button (◀▶) to switch back and forth from exact answers (fractions, roots, π, etc.) and decimal approximations.

The correct answer is 0.428571429.

Example
$\frac{3}{7} =$

[3] ($\frac{n}{d}$) [7] (enter) (◀▶)

If an exact answer is not required, you can press the toggle button (◀▶) immediately to get a decimal approximation from an exact answer without reentering the expression.